# CONTENTS

# CONTENTS CONTINUED

**Acknowledgments**

We would like to acknowledge the help and support from colleagues at NESTA – in particular Michael Harris for his encouragement and perceptive comments on the text. We would also like to thank colleagues from the Young Foundation, especially Yvonne Roberts and Will Norman for their editorial comments and Alex Watson and Sarah Hewes for their contributions.

We are grateful to all those who have provided contributions and guidance, especially Jonathan Gray at The Open Knowledge Foundation, Patrick Andrews of Riversimple and Will Brooks from My Football Club.

This publication represents solely the views of the authors and does not necessarily represent the views of NESTA. Any errors or omissions are those of the authors.

# INTRODUCTION

Ever since its foundation in 1948, the UK's National Health Service has been committed to preventing ill health as well as curing it. Yet, as in other countries, public health remains the Cinderella of the service. It commands less than 2 per cent of NHS resources at a time when obesity, heart disease, mental health and diabetes are all rising steeply. The problem is partly the dominance of curative medicine, and partly fragmented government. How can the NHS influence the multitude of factors contributing to ill health, such as income inequality, unemployment or food policy?

The Bromley-by-Bow Centre, a social venture in London's East End, has pioneered one answer to this problem. It established a healthy living centre that brought together GPs (with a list of 4,200 patients), nurses, arts, education, sheltered housing, support and care and a three acre park. A sculpture in the courtyard welcomes visitors to the centre. The GPs take art classes after work. There is a food co-op whose products the GPs can prescribe for their patients. There is a welfare and benefits advice shop. The centre offers yoga, t'ai chi, aromatherapy, dance classes for children, circuit training for boys and exercise classes for Bengali women, and for older people with arthritis or heart problems.

The centre is based on the common sense principle that what contributes to health is what matters to life itself – friendship, material and emotional security, the chance to express oneself, to feed the spirit, to help and be helped. It is a modern version of the visionary Peckham Health Centre that attempted a radically holistic approach to health in the 1930s. It was closed down in 1948 because of opposition from senior medics. This time round, senior medics and the Government recognise the value of such an approach. The question they have not cracked is what it takes to bring all these services together.

## Social ventures

The Bromley-by-Bow Centre is emblematic of the new social economy. It is a social venture. Like the idea of adventure, from which the word venture derives, a social venture involves a project with an uncertain outcome, whose risk and novelty are part of its attraction. It helps if there are good maps and equipment and the team has within it people with experience and skill. But however well prepared the expedition, its success will always depend on how well it copes with what happens to it along the way. It calls for daring, creativity, and a spirit at ease with uncertainty. Andrew Mawson, the founder of the Bromley-by-Bow Centre, saw a close parallel between venturing in this sense, and the work of artists, which was one of the reasons he insisted that art should be at the heart of the Centre's activities.

Venturing can take place wherever there is a protected space for innovation of this kind. It could be a clinic for low cost cataract operations to address the blindness of 12 million people in India (see **method 1**). Or a patch of desert that Ibrahim Abouleish wanted to transform into an oasis (**method 18**). Or it could be an NHS diabetes centre in Bolton facing an explosion of the condition, or a local Council's initiative in South Tyneside to find new ways to support people on an impoverished housing estate.

## The postal state

Ventures, wherever they take root, are the living centres of the new social economy. Their contemporary significance is that they are the cells of an alternative model of social production to that of 20th century public welfare. The latter was shaped by the organisational innovations of early twentieth century mass production. The principles of scientific management developed by Frederick Winslow Taylor, coupled with the corporate innovations of Alfred Sloane of General Motors, were carried over into the organisation of municipal and Federal government in the United States. In the UK they were pioneered by London Transport in the 1930s and were then adopted as the model for the post-war welfare services and the newly nationalised industries.

The administrative theorist Theo Mars described this as the postal state. It was structured around the delivery of packages – of hospital operations, kilowatts of electricity, or welfare payments to those qualifying for them. Packages of this kind were the product lines of the 20th century state, and they were reflected in the economic territories assigned to the public corporations and to the ministries and departments of government. The postal state was the adequate form for supplying services that could be standardised. The late 20th century public service reforms can in part be understood as trying to extend standardisation and further strengthen the managerial disciplines of the organisational model of mass production.

Yet there are a whole range of problems for which this mass delivery model is ill suited. It finds it difficult to deal adequately with difference and complexity, or with conditions or situations that are difficult to routinise. When problems have multiple causes and require a wide range of inputs from many different sources in order to address them, the service in charge has to cross the chasm that separates administrative and civic territories in order to assemble an integrated solution. As needs become more acute, particularly those requiring emotional support and long term relationships, the cost of the conventional packages rises inexorably. The care industry in the UK is already larger than the car industry. Education and health care, along with care for all ages, account for nearly 20 per cent of domestic production (much more in the US) and are set to grow further.

Above all the postal state is not well equipped to prevent problems arising in the first place. Many of today's most pressing issues – from the rise in obesity and heart disease to domestic and international inequality, the multiplying environmental issues like climate change and the depletion of resources – call for measures that address their root causes not mitigate their results. Structures developed to manage linear chains of production are ill suited to orchestrate complex systems of reduction. For issues such as climate change and good health, systemic sustainability has replaced process efficiency as the primary question to address.

The two key problems with which traditional public organisation is struggling are how to decentralise responsibility on the one hand, and how to integrate such decentralised activity on the other. Studies of living systems are suggestive of models of how this might be done. On the one hand they emphasise the need for distributed systems – systems in which there is a widespread distribution of responsibility for production. Freiburg's buildings covered with solar PV for example are a distributed energy system compared to a large centralised power station. On the other, they focus on mechanisms for linking each node to other parts of the system, allowing them to interconnect through grids, feedback loops, and the distribution of necessary resources.

## Understanding ventures

It is in this context that social ventures have assumed importance. They are nodes of initiative and activity in sustainable systems. But how do they work? What are their key ingredients? What is it that they are able to do that 20th century organisations find so difficult? What goes on beneath the surface of their success?

What is needed is first an understanding of what is already working, an articulation of the approaches they have taken, and the structures and methods they have employed. There is fortunately a growing number of autobiographies and biographies of social entrepreneurs, and collections that gather together the work and achievements of individuals and the organisations they have developed. They are primary sources. Their narratives of achievement are almost all remarkable and inspiring. Many of them read like the lives of the saints or the tales of medieval knights cutting through briars, fighting off dragons, and resisting temptations in order to realise what appears at the outset to be an unapproachable social goal.[1]

It is striking how many of the dragons are so similar: interests threatened by free ambulances, or low cost electricity; bureaucracies defending their existing services; or those with power (like the army) taking over what had been created. But there is also a similar pattern of the 'good forces' attracted to the projects, offering all sorts of support – food, money for the journey, intelligence on paths that avoid the dangers.

Alongside these there is a managerial literature – primarily developed in the United States for what is termed the non-profit sector.[2] This by and large adapts mainstream management literature to non profits. Its focus is on how to raise grant funding and find ways of earning income. There are works on financial control and performance measurement, on competitive strategy and growth, on staff policy and managing organisational change, and on the role of boards and methods of governance when it is social goals rather than private returns that drive the organisation.[3] There has been growing attention recently to the question of how to develop partnerships, networks, and connections with communities, and to the lessons of the methods of private innovation to social innovation.[4]

There is also a great wealth of writing about the management of co-operatives. This is a relatively hermetic literature circulating primarily within the co-operative movement and closely related to a large international network of co-operative colleges – most of the 87 countries in the International Co-operative Alliance have their own specialist colleges, universities or training institutions. There is a strong emphasis on the principles of co-operation and how those are put into practice, through legal forms, governance structures, the involvement of members, the methods of distribution and so on.[5]

Between these two strands of literature – the narrative and the managerial – there is a gulf. Those who have created social ventures do not come over as close readers of the Wiley series on managing not for profits. They have been formed in other ways – often through the church, or through social and political movements, or particular relational professions, like medicine, teaching and social work. This formation takes place off stage as it were, but is critical to understanding the holistic character of the venture and its cultural norms. It is these norms and the way in which ventures create and recreate their cultures that is critical to their success.

The urgency of this inquiry is that if, as we argue, social ventures and their capacity to innovate and integrate are needed as central players in the 21st century economy, we cannot leave the formation of those involved solely to other parts of civil society. The social economy must be able to generate its own actors. Those involved must be able to stand back and make explicit the tacit knowledge which they have brought to the creation of ventures. This collection is in the nature of a first sketch book of some of these issues.

## A living centre

Fortunately the Centre at Bromley-by-Bow is one venture where some of this reflective work has taken place. These include an account by its founder and a study by a team of sociologists to study its work over a three year period. Their aim was to understand why it had proved so successful for people and for an area where so many other initiatives had failed.[6] These reports provide an account of the social and cultural ecology of the venture which has a general relevance to forms of 21st century organisation.

## Inside out

First, the Centre developed organically rather than instrumentally. There was no input-output logic. Rather, it offered conditions which encouraged growth to take place. Germaine Greer who visited the centre called it neither top down nor bottom up but inside out. This is what we mean when we call the project a living centre.[7]

Andrew Mawson's approach was to back enthusiasms. Starting from a church with an elderly congregation of 12, he decided to "leave the windows open and see what flies in". He said yes to everyone who wanted to do something. He gave space and partnered with them to support their projects and connect them into the Centre's growing web of relationships. Nike's slogan 'Just Do It' could equally have applied to Bromley-by-Bow. Many of the projects didn't come off, but many of them did.

This approach, ever more deeply rooted in a particular place, created multiple poles of energy that like a magnet drew volunteers and funds to them. To be successful they had to meet the requirements of any practical production – people with the requisite skills and enthusiasm, an attention to detail, and the creation of services or spaces that had a resonance with users. As the number of projects multiplied, there were more ways in for local residents to engage with the centre and make relationships of their own. It was a form of productive democracy.

## The aesthetic

Andrew Mawson set great store by the physical feel of the Centre's buildings, employing architects and top landscape designers. He covered the walls with art, took down the pulpit in the church and, as a first step in the disability project, invested in a marble suite of toilets.[8] The importance he attached to art in encouraging a spirit of creativity, meant that he welcomed artists to use the centre. He organised numerous art classes and exhibitions and established a gallery at the heart of the healthy living centre.

His account of the centre describes his guiding aesthetic: to be open and alive to possibilities, to back enthusiasms that resonate with the ethic of the centre, and to establish each project and activity on its own sustainable basis. Integral to his approach was the principle of opening up opportunities for people to transform their own lives, and for the Centre to be a place that encourages relationships that affirm 'what it means to be a human being'.

**Reparative creativity**

That was the goal of the Centre. How it was experienced by those who came to the Centre was related by the sociologists. They used a methodology that placed people's biographical narratives at the centre of their study. One person after another described to them a process of personal innovation that mirrored that of the organisation as a whole. Many of those attending had faced all sorts of hardship and trauma. They approached the centre hesitantly, and with a certain vulnerability. The way the centre was designed and run allowed them to rediscover themselves. It encouraged them to do, but it also allowed them to be.

They gave the example of a woman who had become a non speaking recluse after a stroke, but through attending an art class gained confidence in her own creativity, realising that things outside herself could be changed. She went on first to be employed by the centre as a cleaner, then took a Higher National Certificate in Public Arts Management, and finally was promoted to be an artist in residence. The sociologists describe this as 'reparative creativity'. For many it was like a home, and was experienced as a family. The ubiquity of art played a part in this process, as did the precedence given to verbal over written or virtual communications.

**Paths of progression**

The Centre established numerous paths of progression, both for those entering it and those already within. People could start as members (1,400 passed through the centre weekly) and become active in a variety of activities. Some were then promoted to the status of volunteers, not as free labour but as part of the process of active responsibility. They were paid £5 an hour, assigned specific roles and participated in a training programme. From there many were promoted to paid staff roles, or found other jobs through the Centre's networks. The paths were flexible and non-linear. There was a constant switching of roles, of being helped as well as helping others, of teaching and being taught.

These accounts suggest that the model of a living system that encourages social ventures to thrive, works within the venture itself. It is fractal, like a cloud or a coastline. When it is broken down its parts have the same rough shape as the whole, and the parts of its parts similarly. Bromley-by-Bow is a social venture that comprises many social ventures, and each of them has been a vehicle for many personal ventures of individuals who have come to the Centre.

## Management

There are two processes at work here – firstly the seeding of many living centres of initiative and activity, and secondly the creation of the connections that allow them to flourish. As it has grown the centre has become a mosaic of activities that can be tapped into by any of the ventures. Its resources and support can be assembled round individuals and their initiatives rather than being institutionally determined and allocated on the basis of classification.

The role of management of a system of this kind is quite different to that of delivery organisations. It is in part establishing the organisation and its ethos, what we have called its aesthetic – its openness, its creativity, and the primacy given to the fostering of relationships. In part it is to support and guide the projects as they arise and help them connect internally and externally. But it is also to act as a container and resolver of tensions.

These roles change over time. The sociologists observed that there was an initiatory phase that was pioneering, creative, going it alone, abrasive, and navigating without charts. This was followed by a reparative phase that required slow relational work to manage the many tensions that emerged as the Centre grew. Finally, there was a period of evolution, in which the need to sustain and manage the existing activities, was balanced by the drive for further innovation and expansion.

Leadership at first was that of the pioneer. By the reparative phase it had split into three parts: an outward looking role, a financial role concerned with raising funds and internal financial management, and an operational role which was focussed on the containment of the tensions and the nurturing of an integrative internal culture. For a time these roles were played by three different people. Later they were combined in one. To these should be added numerous project and supplementary leadership roles. The sociologists referred to this as 'systemic co-entrepreneurship'.[9]

The management of tensions was central. They were the necessary tensions of integration. In the model of integrated working on which the Healthy Living Centre was based there were tensions between health professionals and the community and art workers. In the Centre as a whole there were tensions between old and young, between conservation and innovation, between the many different ethnic groups who used the centre and between the need for a safe haven and the anxieties generated as the result of the community business model. How these tensions were contained and used as a trigger for further innovation is a key part of the story.

### Chaordic organisation

The Centre at Bromley-by-Bow is similar to many social and environmental ventures in its open-ended and multidimensional form of development. Such ventures bundle together things that have traditionally been separated – in the environmental field the management of water, waste, electricity and telematics for example. They pursue ecological and social goals through the same project, and spin off new initiatives that realise their goals in unexpected ways.

These forms of chaordic organisation – both chaotic and ordered – face severe constraints within hierarchical rule based structures such as those that have been shaped to deliver standard welfare packages.[10] Yet it is their capacity to mobilise widely distributed initiative, energy and resources, and to integrate them around multi-faceted problems that is required for many of the most intractable of our contemporary problems.

### Social ventures as integrators of economies

Social ventures are core elements of a new model of the social economy, which transects the state, the market, and the complex web of households and the informal economy. Social ventures provide a way of bringing these other economies together in ways which large-scale, rule-based organisations find extremely difficult.

Ventures like Bromley-by-Bow raise some money from the state – and indeed in their case have located at the heart of the centre one of the principal institutions of formal public health care – a GP's surgery.[11] They have raised grants, and at the same time promoted social enterprises that sell their services on the market. What they have also done – which is so difficult for large rule-based organisations – is to create a place and a culture which is experienced as an extension of the household and attracts large numbers of local people on those terms. Mutual caring, reciprocity and a sense of the common good that are features of the household economy are also to be found in many social ventures.

## Understanding the social

The venture at Bromley-by-Bow is a story of the work of a charismatic leader and his successors, and of the complex social and cultural organisation that emerged. It is the social and cultural aspects of successful social ventures that are often taken for granted but which we particularly need to understand. They are at the very heart of the distinctiveness of social ventures. They shape their goals, and generate their energy. They provide cohesiveness that elsewhere rests on financial incentives and formal structures. For social ventures, the forms of ownership, payment, management structures, and policies on distribution must be shaped to reflect the venture's culture not erode it.

The literature on these issues is thinner. The psycho-social intelligence of the sociologists in the Bromley-by-Bow study is rare for work on social ventures but not for the worlds of work and welfare. To take only one example, the Tavistock Clinic, founded in 1920, in the aftermath of shell shock in the First World War, has a long tradition of applying therapeutic approaches to social issues. Through the separate Tavistock Institute, it has also had a major impact on organisational theory and practice. One of the Clinic's tools, known as work discussion, focuses on learning from experience through close observation of work situations, and developing interpretations of the experiences with those involved. This has the potential to help with the work and methods of social ventures.[12]

Another suggestive body of writing is that from within and about the new social movements. Social movements have been major sources of social innovation and its diffusion through a number of different pathways. They have generated their own ventures that have provoked changes within the market and the state. They have had an impact on consumers, and the resulting changes in demand have been transmitted through retailers to commercial producers. And they have had a broader political impact on the fiscal and regulatory framework of the economy as a whole.[13] They are, in short, significant players in the modern economy.

A prominent theme of the literature from within social movements is the qualitative nature of the economy. The food and environmental movements, for example, or the campaigns on health and housing have their own extensive literature on economic alternatives in their actual and desired form.

Much of this is structured round case studies. For these movements case studies play a critical role – as symbolic representations that prefigure systemic innovation on the one hand, and as material proof that 'another way is possible' on the other. They act as mobilising exemplars, and while many have been formed and driven forward by inspiring individuals the emphasis in these cases tends to focus on the qualitative character of the project and the many who have contributed to its making.

The work about (rather than from within) the new movements looks at them as social and political phenomena and is concerned above all with how culture is formed. It focuses on the development of shared ideas and conceptual worlds. It involves what the anthropologist Gregory Bateson terms the common framing of issues, that in turn generates an agreed diagnostic of the present and a shared perspective of the future.[14] Particular attention is paid to relationships and identities, and how these are constructed and strengthened through collaborative activities (of special relevance for those in the social economy working with marginalised groups such as adolescents or minorities whose segregated identities are not affirmed by others).

From this perspective social movements are cultural enterprises whose goals, organisational forms and processes have a wider cultural resonance. They have their own narratives and means of story telling, their own symbolic initiatives, and collective events. While they have acknowledged leaders (often with a magical quality), their members also act as part of a wider distributed leadership in respect to local operations and to the extension of the movement as a whole.

Understanding the cultural components of social movements will be particularly relevant for a subsequent collection in this series on the scaling of social innovation and systemic change. For the micro issue of venture formation, the importance of this literature is that it connects what may appear as a narrower managerial project to currents of intellectual analysis – sociology, psychoanalysis, cultural studies, anthropology – that have particular bearing on social ventures. For these are ventures in which culture is a central organising principle both in the way they operate and in the services themselves. Many social ventures provide relational services – in care, or health or education for example – where issues of trust, anxiety, motivation, creativity and the containment and resolution of conflict are all critical for the quality and effectiveness of the service.[15]

## The collection

This collection is a first contribution to the much larger task of pulling together the many methods used across the social economy. We have not covered the mainstream business methods that can be adopted by social ventures, since these are widely available. Nor have we included the methods and strategies for incorporating innovations within the public sector into the mainstream organisational and budgetary process. These will be the subject of separate volumes. Rather we have chosen a number of issues which the experience of the authors suggest have been valuable in establishing social ventures on a sound footing.

What we explore are those things that are distinctive characteristics of social ventures. There are four that bear on many of the issues covered:

i)   A venture driven by a social mission has an interest in maximising the spread of an innovation beyond the level dictated by the venture's own financial interest. This leads to a common tension: between on the one hand an interest in collaboration and the free diffusion of ideas and know-how determined by the mission, and on the other an interest in restriction determined by the interest of the financial survival of the organisation. It is the art of the business model to find a way for ventures to do both, to remain open and collaborative while surviving financially. Often it is this very openness and readiness to share information and know-how that generates income in roundabout ways. What goes round comes round. It is one of the things those with a mainstream commercial background find counterintuitive that a venture can gain financially by giving things away.

ii)  A social venture, because of its social mission, attracts the voluntary. The principles of a gift economy – gifts in the form of cash, of time, of know-how and resources – supplant those of a transactional economy. It is as if the magnetic pole of the commercial economy suddenly switches direction, so that instead of self interest being the motive force, it is the interest of others that becomes the force of attraction. A gift economy has its own obligations and complexities, and one of the challenges of a social venture is how to manage the two economies simultaneously, the volunteer working beside the wage worker, the venture seeking donations at the same time as finding ways to earn its own income, managing prices that may carry within them the elements of a gift.

iii) A social venture has most to gain from being an open system for both of the above reasons, yet this is easier said than done. Ventures are subject to the day-to-day disciplines of keeping the show on the road. They tend to turn inwards behind their organisational moat. The idea pulls one way, the daily practice another.

iv) Centralised versus distributed control. The forces underlying the contest between hierarchy and heterarchy – a theme of the organisational transformation of commercial business over the past 25 years – are compounded in the social economy.[16] In addition to the issues of information and creativity that have underpinned the trends to flatter and networked organisations in the private market, the social economy has the additional factor of motivating the voluntary and reflecting the relational qualities of the venture's principles in the job design and responsibility of all those involved.

There is no way of escaping or resolving these tensions, but as we have seen with the Bromley-by-Bow Centre there are ways of containing and managing them productively, so that the values and goals of the ventures remain primary.

The methods that follow, written as they are on the basis of the ventures with which the authors have been involved, are necessarily partial. They should be read as methods that have been beta tested but not codified. They are an invitation for others to contribute additional and alternative methods that they have found useful, which can be included in subsequent collections in this series and on the website that accompanies it.

End notes

1   Examples are listed in the bibliography.
2   The US literature is now substantial. The American publisher Wiley has a publication list with more than 400 volumes on managing non profits.
3   A useful entry point to this literature is J. Gregory Dees, Jed Emerson and Peter Economy, Strategic Tools for Social Entrepreneurs, Wiley 2002.
4   This is one of the themes in the work of the Innovation Network for Communities in the United States. See for example their founding document: The Innovation Network for Communities – A Framework for Accelerating Place-Based Social Innovation September 2007 www.nupolis.com.
5   See for example W P Watkins Co-operative Principles – Today and Tomorrow, Co-op College 1990.
6   Lynn Froggett, Prue Chamberlayne, Tom Wengraf and Stef Buckner, Integrated Practice – focus on older people, Report of the Bromley-by-Bow Centre research and evaluation project, University of Central Lancashire and Open University, 2005.
7   The idea of living centres has been developed for buildings by the architect Christopher Alexander (see **method 4**).
8   Japanese electronic manufacturers establishing themselves on the US East Coast, screened potential sub contractors by first visiting their toilets and restaurants whose condition and distinctions of rank they saw as reflecting the respect paid by management to their workers.
9   A key role through many stages of the orga nisation's development was played by Dr Sam Everington. He had the medical knowledge that lay at the heart of a project focused on health, and was also himself a quietly brilliant public and social entrepreneur. Where Andrew Mawson had the charismatic, and often abrasive qualities that make social entrepreneurs successful in getting projects off the ground, Sam Everington exemplifies the skills that are vital in making projects sustainable, including the ability to learn from mistakes.
10  The term chaordic organisation is that of Dee Hock, the founder of Visa. He sees it as reflecting the fundamental organising principles of nature, blending apparent opposites such as co-operation and competition, self-organisation and coherence, freedom and concern for the common good. See his One From Many, Berrett-Koehler 2005.
11  Part of their success came from becoming very adept at securing funding from government and other public agencies – which sometimes caused resentment amongst others in the area.
12  See Margaret Rustin and Jonathan Bradley, Work Discussion: Learning from Reflective Practice in Work with Children and Families, Karnac 2008. This contains a number of illuminating case studies, whose significance extends well beyond schools, hospitals and care homes that are the primary sites of discussion.
13  Interestingly it is a Professor of Organisational Behaviour at Stanford University's Business School who has noted the significance of social movements for the market economy. Hayagreeva Rao in his Market Rebels, Princeton University Press 2009, argues that enthusiasts construct 'hot causes' that arouse intense emotions, and use unconventional techniques – what he calls 'cool mobilisation' – to engage audiences in collective action. He illustrates this with the motor enthusiasts who trialled what in effect were prototypes, and pressed for regulatory changes that made wide car use possible. They created the conditions for Ford's Model T. He shows how the real ale and nouvelle cuisine movements changed their respective sectors, as did those resisting bio-technological pharmaceuticals.

14   The late Antonio Melucci, who was both a sociologist and psychotherapist, remains one of the most perceptive writers on new social movements. See his Nomads of the Present, Radius, 1989, The Playing Self, Cambridge University Press 1996, and Challenging Codes: collective action in the information age, Cambridge University Press 1996. See also Alaine Touraine, The voice and the eye: An analysis of social movements. Cambridge University Press 1981, and Part 3 chapter 2 in his Critique of Modernity, Blackwell, 1995. There is a useful summary of social movement theory and its application to organisational change in a public service by Paul Bate, Helen Bevan and Glenn Robert, Towards a Million Change Agents: A review of the social movements literature: implications for large scale change in the NHS, NHS Modernisation Agency, 2005.

15   The Tavistock Clinic has a long tradition using psychoanalytic theory and techniques to understand organisations, and inform the policy and practice of social welfare. Their series published by Karnac has a great deal of relevance for those engaged in social ventures, see for example, Clare Huffington (ed) Working Below the Surface: the emotional life of contemporary organisations, Karnac 2004, and Andrew Cooper and Julian Lousada, Borderline Welfare, Karnac 2005.

16   The term heterarchy is that of Gerard Fairclough, a bio chemist who was CEO of Shell Chemicals, and then the founder and CEO of Celltech, the leading bio-pharmaceutical company in the UK. He defines it as multiple rule, a balance of powers rather than the single rule of a hierarchy. He further distinguishes it from responsible autonomy where a group decides what to do but is responsible for its outcome. See his book, The Three Ways of Getting Things Done, Triarchy Press, 2005.

# SECTION 1: THE PROCESS OF VENTURE FORMATION

After successful prototyping and testing, launching the service or product on a sustainable basis involves the development of an economic model that will secure its financial future.

In the case of a public sector innovation this requires integrating it into the central budgetary process. It means evidence and tactics specific to the public sector, where, with respect to core services, it is less a question of finding new sources of finance, than of transforming or replacing existing services. But to move from pilots and prototypes to a securely established public innovation, it is often advisable to set it up as a separate venture, with public finance and a service contract that can prove itself at scale.

The service itself becomes an independent social venture, with all the issues that such a venture entails. Launching a venture involves six key things:

- a business model that runs parallel to the core idea of the venture and which sets out how it can become sustainable

- a governance model, what the Mondragon co-operative network calls sovereignty, that provides a clear map of control and accountability, as well as protective safeguards (not least to protect it from predators if the project is a success)

- sources of finance – both start-up/equity funding and income streams over time

- a network and communications model to develop what we refer to as the venture's relational capital

- a staffing model including the role of volunteers

- a development plan for operational systems – including management information, reporting and financial systems, IT, supply chain systems (logistics, transparency, quality control) and systems for risk management

These will be translated into an economic or business plan, which details the service or initiative, how it will be provided, by whom, with what inputs, how much it will cost and how it will generate income.

# 1 BUSINESS MODELS

Generating an idea, prototyping and then testing it, is one thing. Launching it into the wide sea of the economy is quite another. Every initiative requires a proposition about its economic seaworthiness. This is its business model – the strategic concept for the project's financial sustainability.[1] It is the economic idea that runs parallel to the social idea around which the project revolves.

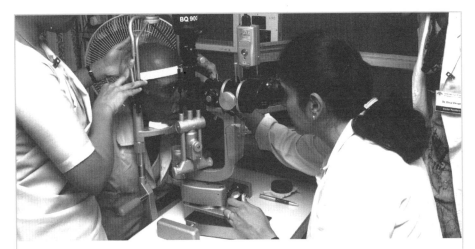

Govindappa Venkataswamy was the son of a farmer who became an eye surgeon. Inspired by Gandhi, he was appalled that over 12 million Indians were blind, 80 per cent because of cataracts for which they couldn't afford the treatment. So after retirement in 1976 and inspired by Japanese and US industrial models, he set out to 'eradicate needless blindness' by developing a new system for sight-saving cataract surgeries.

The Aravind system uses physicians' time only on activities that require their particular skills (they can now do 2,000 operations a year against the national average of 220). Other tasks are left to ophthalmic technicians. Organisational systems ensure the optimal use of operating theatres. Mass 'eye camps' screen prospective patients and transport them for surgery the same afternoon. The principle of flow as applied to eye surgery means that his five main hospitals in Tamil Nadu and Pondicherry carry out 175,000 cataract surgeries and some 100,000 other eye surgeries and laser procedures a year.

This is one part of his social business model. The other is his principle of pricing. Two thirds of all patients receive their treatment for free, or at steeply subsidised rates. But the sheer volume of operations keeps costs so low ($10 as against $1,700 in the US) that those paying for the operation pay a lower price than if the service was restricted to them alone. As a result, the Aravind system has never depended on donations or grants. Its 'profits' are re-invested in the latest technology and the expansion of the service.

## Private market business models

The market is a bran tub of business models. Henry Ford's was the principle of mass production coupled with a wage of $5 a day that would create a core market to buy the cars. General Motors introduced the concept of design-led model changes. Sam Walton built Wal-Mart on the principle of tiny margins and large volumes. McDonalds added to the principle of mass production the idea of franchising and the standard modularisation of its outlets (the company can complete the construction of a drive-through within nine days). Tupperware was based on pyramid home selling. Gillette sold its razors cheap and made money on the blades (the bait and hook model). Delta Airlines adopted a hub and spoke (instead of point to point) system for its airlines, and FedEx adopted a similar model for freight and became the largest airline in the world.

Toyota took 30 years to develop its Just in Time production system (pulling production through in response to demand rather than pushing it through as in mass production) and inspired an industrial revolution. Dell used this principle to assemble its computers to order, cut out the retailers by telephone and online selling, and became the largest computer sales company in the world within 15 years. Benetton adopted Just in Time dyeing of garments in response to electronic sales data from its shops. Ryanair revolutionised air transport by slashing fares and making up its income from website advertising plus cash payments from regional airports who were ready to pay for the visitors.

All these are examples of innovative business models that have been widely copied and have transformed their industries. They combine material ideas about the product or service (the kind of hamburger or the quality of the razor) and an economic proposition about how each is produced and distributed. The two are interwoven. Ryanair's link of provincial cities (the service) means they can ask for cash inducements from provincial governments.

The social economy needs to keep a close eye on the market's transformative innovations. Dr Venkataswamy wanted to market good eyesight to the world in the way McDonalds sells hamburgers. He was inspired by a visit to the McDonalds factory in the US. The National Health Service (NHS) set up NHS Direct on the model of private call centres and is now applying Japanese 'lean production' techniques to hospital organisation.

## Social economy business models

There are three distinct features of the social economy which call for it to have innovative business models of its own. First, much of the social economy is focussed on those who cannot afford market-based services, and on services that it is difficult or undesirable to commodify. This means that revenue from sales may contribute little if at all to the necessary income. Put more generally, if the social goal is to maximise the spread of a service, any price is likely to act as a restriction. The Aravind system found a way round this, but could do so only because of the standardised nature of its service.

Second, if the goal is to maximise the spread of a service, a social organisation should by its nature be non proprietorial. Far from restricting its know-how and skills within the castle walls of ownership it has an interest in diffusing them to others in the social economy. This puts a question mark beside potential income to be earned from a project's intellectual property and the sale of its skills.

Third, the way in which services are produced, and how they are distributed and income is raised, has a bearing on what is voluntarily contributed. There is a moral economy which is distinct from that of an economy bound together by market transactions (whether for inputs, labour, finance or sales).

The methods of production and of revenue raising should be in tune with the social idea of the service. The methods are the message (or at least part of it). Using slave labour in cocoa plantations in francophone Africa is not the basis for a fair trade chocolate. In this sense the business model should provide part of the magnetic attraction of the project. Like the social idea it needs to be simple, feasible and arresting.

From one perspective these characteristics may appear to tie a social venture's economic hands behind its back and put it at a disadvantage vis a vis the conventional market. But they equally confer their own distinct advantages that in many cases have been decisive in social economic success.

## Social enterprise business models

### Brands
Take fair trade for example. A number of different business models have been tried out with varied results. In continental Europe fair trade grew under the umbrella of a fair trade mark (the Max Havelaar mark in Holland was the first in 1988) but lost some of its resilience in the face of competition from lower standard marks. UK fair trade companies have framed their business models around a brand (Cafédirect, Divine, Equal Exchange, Liberation, Peopletree and Traidcraft for example) and have been better able to deal with the competitive challenge from mainstream companies that have adopted the fair trade label.

**Supermarket sourcing**

In France the fair trade company Altereco followed a different path. It set out to become a specialist sourcing company for supermarkets' own label fair trade products.

**Social retailing**

In Italy, the leading fair trade importer, CTM, is owned by a network of 250 co-operative fair trade shops, and acts as their supplier of fair trade products. Traidcraft in the UK has likewise grown in part through a network of church groups whom it supplies via a mail order catalogue. Oxfam's fair trade engagement principally revolves around its network of shops.

The advantage of the social retailer model is that in the CTM case each of the 250 shops becomes a node of largely voluntary local advocacy. It is also a ready source of finance (see **method 15**). The same is the case with Traidcraft and of Oxfam, and their wide network of volunteers and promoters.

## Producer oriented intermediaries

The producer-oriented companies like Twin Trading (the fair trader that initiated Cafédirect, Divine and Liberation) or the Dutch based fresh fruit company Agrofair have based their market proposition on the strength of their social idea (their close long term partnerships with small farmer producer co-operatives). The challenge for their business model is that the costs of the intensive relationships involved, and their assumption of trading risks normally shouldered by the primary producers, means that their cost structure is higher than mainstream arms length traders.

Twin Trading's business model has been to supply on an exclusive basis the fair trade marketing companies who establish their differentiation in the market through their brands. As fair trade has grown, Twin Trading faces a dilemma. It can continue its exclusive supply agreements. Or it can become a general supplier to all fair trade marketing companies, including supermarkets, and develop its own intermediate brand – like an Intel inside, or Dolby Stereo – to show its difference from mainstream traders. Or it could break up its functions into packages of particular fair trade services to support fair trade supply chain management by mainstream companies entering the field.

These are examples of the choice of business models open to social enterprises in a single sector. In the case of fair trade it is a sector comprising traders rather than producers. The business models differ in the way in which they relate to producers, to retailers and to consumers and the degree to which these relations (e.g. via supermarkets) allow them to realise their social goals.

Given that supermarkets require margins of between 30 per cent and 55 per cent on fair trade goods, one of the major challenges for the fair traders is how to persuade supermarkets to accept lower margins (as the French fair trader Ethiquable has done and announce it on their packaging) or to develop alternative lower margin sales routes, for example through mail order or in the case of Altertrade in Japan, through large scale co-operative home delivery box schemes.

Such commodity producing social enterprises stand at one end of a spectrum, since they have commodities or services which they sell on the market. Depending on their purposes (and their efficiency) they can make a social distribution of some of their surplus (to the producers in the case of fair trade or to the street sellers in the case of the Big Issue). The general point here is that there is a market within which such enterprises seek to fashion out an alternative.

## Landed property and rent

There are sectors where the issues are quite different: those ventures which are concerned with landed property and rent for example, whether the settling and support of the rural landless, or the development of low cost housing, or office space (as with the Oxford based Ethical Property Company) or of integrated developments such as Coin Street community builders on the South Bank in London, or Lynedoch in South Africa (see **method 2**).

## Manufacturing and service producers

Or there are production ventures like the many social service co-ops in Italy or manufacturers like the social and ecological shoe companies (the Soul of Africa is an example in South Africa that covenants all its profits to those suffering from AIDS).

In all these cases – and in those ventures that rely primarily on grants and donations – a business model is a necessary starting point if an innovative idea is to become a sustainable venture.

> The business concepts of the social economy require as much care and creativity in their generation as the social ideas. The two are best developed together to sustain and re-enforce each other. For social enterprises, the business model represents a strategy for sustainability. It needs to be simple, persuasive and striking, since along with the social idea, it is a key part of a venture's attraction. Its impact comes from showing how a social idea can be realised in practice and sustained economically. Business models that work are themselves a prime area for social innovation.

Links

http://files.businessmodeldesign.com/publications/The%20Business%20Model%20Ontology%20a%20proposition%20in%20a%20design%20science%20approach.pdf
http://www.altromercato.it/en

Reading

Johanna Mair and Oliver Schoen "Successful social entrepreneurial business models in the context of developing economies" International Journal of Emerging Markets Vol. 2 No. 1, 2007 pp. 54-68

End notes

1   This is a narrower definition than is commonly used for commercial business models. We want to highlight the core economic idea in a social venture business model, since it is this rather than the more detailed elaboration of the various elements of the business that complement's the venture's social idea and acts as a pole of attraction.

# 2 INCOMES AND OUTCOMES

A common challenge to social ventures is how they finance the gap between their necessary costs and what they can earn by any direct sales on the market. How do they maximise services to those who cannot afford market prices, and provide services for which the market is ill suited while at the same time sustaining themselves financially?

The Lynedoch EcoVillage is the first ecologically designed, socially mixed intentional community in South Africa. It is located in the wine country near Stellenbosch, 30 minutes drive inland from Cape Town. The initial business model could not raise sufficient capital to cover the eco-innovation and facilitation processes that were central to the project. So the founders separated the project's eco-social development dimension from its property development side.

The first step was a school, funded by the Government, with 475 places serving the families of local farm workers. For pre-school children they built a Montessori kindergarten. They then partnered with the nearby Stellenbosch University, to establish a Sustainability Institute in a converted hotel in the centre of the village. The Institute runs a Masters course in sustainable development, whose practical projects and related research programme focus on the village, and provide the ecological research and community development support for the project.

What to the banks and local authorities appeared an unsustainable overhead, was shifted into a research and educational economy based on fees and grant funding. It has even inspired a UK-based entrepreneur, Sally Wilton, to open an eco-cinema in Kensal Rise, London, whose profits go to fund the Lynedoch Institute.

Restructured in this way, the property development finance was forthcoming. An ecological infrastructure has been laid down and 35 houses are now completed in Phase 1 (40 per cent of them subsidized through a Government programme). The new owners have formed a Home Owners Association to run the village and guide its second stage.

There are six approaches to generating income to fund outcomes that cannot be realised through the market:

### i) Radical technical and organisational change

Transformations of production enable redistribution. They generate a surplus that can be redistributed through cheap or free services. In the environmental field there are many such initiatives that aim at Factor Four gains, ones that double output at half the cost. In the social sphere the Aravind system exemplifies the same principle. In this case the service is sold on the market. But it also applies to public services, and the ability of social ventures (generated from within or from outside the state sphere) to provide Factor Four public services. An example is Elderpower in Maine which is developing a model of improved services that can be adopted for publicly funded care of the elderly and cuts its cost by a factor of seven.[1]

### ii) Disaggregating the package

This is the model adopted by the Lynedoch EcoVillage, and recognises that different parts of a venture can be sustained through different economies. Some parts can generate goods and services that can be sold on the market. Others are services or outcomes that attract public or foundation funds. Still others can appeal to individual subscriptions and donations. There is a guiding principle here of hypothecated funding.

Another version of the same idea is to disaggregate by time. Initial R&D and exploratory production can be funded through grants or sales to a premium market until the service achieves a form and quality and costs are reduced sufficiently for them to be affordable for individuals or for Governments to fund on a long term basis. This is the approach adopted by the Green Homes smart energy advice service in London.

### iii) Capturing the rent created by the venture

Regeneration projects raise the value of landed property in an area – through improved schooling and healthcare for example, or housing and transport. Some projects start with improved retailing, and recently with the laying of a digital infrastructure. Whatever the strategy, the key for financing – as with all private property development – is the capturing of the increased ground rent that results, preferably by securing the freehold of as much property as possible that will be affected by the project, commonly in a land trust. Lynedoch's model takes this into account by the project receiving some of the increased value of the housing when it is sold on by its owners.

## iv) Capturing the full value of the tangible assets

Just as there may be underused public assets, so a venture may find many uses for its own tangible assets. Stirling City Council created the post of a film officer who was stationed in Hollywood and attracted a number of films to be made in Stirling. Many social buildings, swimming pools, and forests have features that can be used in lateral ways – from locations for shoots, to destinations for those studying social innovation.

## v) Free service business models

One approach is to get free inputs on the basis that there will be free outputs. This is the model of food banks in North America, where retailers and companies donate surplus stock for free distribution (largely through voluntary labour) to those in need. It is also the underlying principle of open source projects based on distributed collaboration. Project Gutenberg, for example, uses volunteers to scan and proof tens of thousands of out of copyright books for free distribution on the web. ClimatePrediction.net works on a similar principle, using volunteers' computers to model the earth's climate. In each of these there is an irreducible link between voluntary inputs and freely accessible outputs.

## vi) Tapping the value of a network: lessons from the web

Many social ventures develop extensive networks – not least the users of the venture's free services. The development of the web has greatly increased the range and scope of these networks. Much can be learnt from the private web economy, which has seen free services create large audiences, and has been developing business models that capture the economic value of these audiences.

There have been the following private market strategies:

- for virtual market sites like eBay or Craigslist, or indeed for many information businesses like lastminute.com, a small cut can be taken from each transaction, the revenue coming not from access to the website but from the use of the site for monetary transactions

- the costs of maintaining a site can be cut by the low cost generation of content (notably through user generated content in sites like Facebook or YouTube)

- monetising the value of the audience, principally through website advertising or selling market information on users analysed from their use of the site

Whereas commercial sites are now being pressed to place maximising revenue above maximising the audience, social economy websites put maximising their audience above maximising their revenue.[2] But they still need 'sufficient' revenue to operate. Take, for example, openDemocracy or Pambazuka News. OpenDemocracy is an online thrice-weekly journal of international current affairs. It has 150,000 regular readers worldwide, 3.5 million unique visitors and 1 million repeat viewings. Pambazuka News is a weekly newsletter on human rights in Africa, based on user generated content (60 per cent of it from Africa) with a readership of 0.5 million. The interest of both these publications is in as wide a readership as possible. Charging to access either of them would threaten to dramatically reduce their readership.

## Lessons from the online economy

Online sites – because of their reach – pose a question relevant to all social ventures namely how the network they create can realise the value of its own aggregation. There are the following possibilities:

i. **Discounts on purchases.** A large audience has power as a collective purchaser. The Green Communities in Canada, for example, negotiated discounts on selected items like low energy boilers because of the wide coverage of its programme. In this case the social intermediary was acting for consumers rather than as an intermediary for the supplying firms. By identifying approved products, it would then approach the supplying firms for discounts on the grounds that it was offering the suppliers a saving on their marketing and sales expenditures to reach this audience. Amazon is currently offering social organisations (including openDemocracy) a cut from feed-ins to Amazon but these margins are small.

ii. **Access to the audience.** Advertising is the most common form of charging for access, and is the basis for Google's rise to being the largest advertising medium in the world. Social organisations are understandably reluctant to take advertisements because it runs counter to the spirit of the social relationships on which the project is based. But they can advertise their own paid for services (like events) or goods (like books) and there are almost always some complementary organisations whose messages support the work of the project and the interests of its audience without compromising either. It may be a municipality wishing to advertise its energy efficiency scheme or a local festival. The Green Communities in Canada discovered the value of their own home visit programme when local councils paid half the cost of the home visits in return for the visitor taking five minutes to explain municipal programmes and offers.

iii. **The audience selling information about itself.** Websites and credit card companies are two of the many types of business that sell information about their users for marketing purposes. A social audience can turn this on its head and selectively sell its own information. For example, a group of NHS patients could undertake a study of themselves and sell the results to a Primary Care Trust.

iv. **The freemium model.** This involves providing the basic service for free and charging for premium services or for applications of the service. This is what has happened with Linux, which provides the basic code as part of its free open source package, but other companies like Red Hat have sprung up that develop and sell applications of the code. For social organisations the offer could be hands on advice and the application of the freely circulated knowledge (this is the business model adopted by Livemocha. com for its language learning, which has a free language school supplemented by a paid for premium service).

v. **Associated enterprises.** Many social organisations have income earning initiatives that run parallel to their free service. They may run conferences and events, or an associated publishing house, like Pambazuka News. They can offer consultancy services on the basis of their specialised knowledge of content and also of the information system that they have developed. Each of these is a form of mini-social enterprise that can use the free website as a medium of contact with a wide audience.

vi. **Support payments for the free service.** There are organisations and individuals who have an interest in a service reaching a wide audience by remaining free. They can donate in the form of a voluntary subscription. In some cases it is individual as with National Public Radio in the US. In others it is collective. For example libraries have formed consortia to jointly fund the costs of providing open access to scholarly publications. There are also pledge subscriptions in which people pledge to pay for a free service if a certain number of others do as well.

Social websites are only one example of a venture which is centred round providing a free service, but it has lessons for many social organisations that face the quandary of how to ensure that their service is free while raising enough finance to sustain themselves. This is where some of the methods used in the virtual world have wider relevance, not least because any social venture – school, hospital, or care charity – now needs to have a strong web presence itself. They, too, have a challenge to create an audience of supporters, and to find ways of raising income by accessing the value of that audience in ways that are consistent with the values of the service.

## The double helix

We distinguish the social idea behind an innovation from the business concept that will enable it to become a sustainable venture. In the best cases the economic innovation is intertwined with the social in a double helix. Curitiba's idea of paying for waste rather than charging for it was simultaneously an economic and a social innovation. The Aravind Eye Care System was able to offer free eye surgery to the poor through its radical transformation of the surgical process.

In other cases there is a tension between the social and the economic, between maximising the spread of a service and finding a means to pay for it. Business models address this second issue. They should be developed with as much imagination as the original social concept and re-enforce the project's attraction of goodwill and support.

There are a range of social business models that involve recognising the potential value of a venture's assets – tangible and intangible – and disaggregating its activities to generate alternative income streams. Particularly instructive for social ventures are the lessons from the business models adopted by web companies which, like social ventures, have an interest in maintaining free access, while at the same time generating revenues indirectly as the result of the response that the free service attracts.

Links
www.greenhomeslondon.co.uk

End notes

1   For a host of other environmental examples see Ernst von Weizsacker, Amory Lovins and L.Hunter Lovins, Factor Four, Earthscan, 1997.

2   Deloitte Media Predictions 2009. A review of the 'private' social network economy concluded:

> *Social networks need to consider how to transform themselves in 2009. Management at social networks must be able to demonstrate a desire and ability to monetise subscribers. It should also effect a change of culture within the workforce so that it focuses on revenues not just subscribers. Investors should take a hard line, but be radical in their thinking on the monetisation issue. Monetising social interaction when it used to be free is hard. But if members are hard to monetise, the focus may need to shift to generating revenues from the aggregate value of their actions and behaviour.*

Sites with professional content like newspapers are among the first to look to charging models (led by Rupert Murdoch). Of the 7 major UK dailies (who together had 140 million unique users of their online services in January 2009) none as yet charge, though the Financial Times charges for its online version at half the rate of its print subscription and has 110,000 subscribers for what is a specialist daily.

# 3 CHARTING THE ELEMENTS

Once an idea has been worked up and prototyped, what is necessary to ensure that it can be economically and socially sustained? The first answer is usually money, but there are many other factors that are needed besides money and which are often a condition for raising successive tranches of finance.

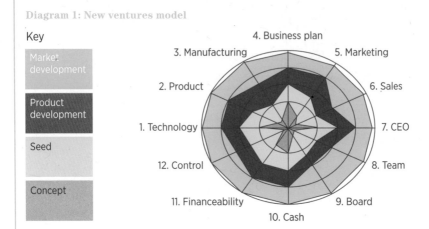

Diagram 1: New ventures model

Key
- Market development
- Product development
- Seed
- Concept

4. Business plan
3. Manufacturing
5. Marketing
2. Product
6. Sales
1. Technology
7. CEO
12. Control
8. Team
11. Financeability
9. Board
10. Cash

Social venturing is often equated with social entrepreneurs. This parallels the genius theory of venture capital in Silicon Valley. For venture capitalists the dictum has been, 'find a genius and build a business around him or her'.

It was in reaction to this that two Silicon Valley-ers Gordon Bell and Heidi Mason developed a method for analysing start-ups and mapping their progress which was not dependent on what they called 'highly caffeinated, insomniac heroes'.

Their model for new ventures has 12 axes shown in the diagram above. For each of them progress is mapped in four stages. First is the concept stage. This is seeded and then developed as a product. Finally there is the market development stage. They have used this diagnostic model to chart the progress of more than 450 ventures, in order to identify key areas for further development so that one of them does not bring the whole project down.

In the diagram the most progress has been made along the technology axis (as we might expect in Silicon Valley), along with the business plan, the CEO and the financing axes. The least developed are sales, the team, the Board, and systems of control. For the social economy the issues of control, the team and relations with users are likely to have greater priority and may in fact be the substance of a new social technology on which a venture is based.

As in Silicon Valley, many environmental ventures start with technology, or rather with the absence of a particular material or process. It may be a question of developing dry cleaning methods which don't use chlorine, or a textile process that does not pollute. Similarly there are social ventures that involve material innovations such as new software systems or disability aids.

But many social and environmental ventures are primarily concerned with social technology. Their innovations are in the economic and social ways in which services are produced and distributed. The introduction of personal health coaches on the NHS for example is not a material technology. There is a well established profession of private health coaches. The innovation is extending their remit to those with chronic disease as an alternative to more conventional forms of health care.

In such cases the diagnostic tool for social ventures will start not from a technology or product, but from the user or 'community of benefit' as it is sometimes called. The user is an active participant in the project, not a consumer to be 'sold to'. Often, as in health care, it is a question of finding an alternative process or treatment for a particular person rather than developing a process that is 'marketed' widely. A new method is then diffused through organisational and social networks rather than being patented and marketed by the innovator.

## Axes

There are in short additional axes and different starting points for social and environmental ventures to those used to monitor a Silicon Valley venture. This is illustrated in diagram 2. Here we have merged the Bell-Mason axes of technology and manufacturing with the product or service (axis 2 in diagram 2), and highlight instead the 'community of benefit' (axis 1). This is the pole of orientation for so many social ventures – for social co-ops employing those with disabilities for example, or for innovations in birthing and child care. The community of benefit may be co-designers, co-producers or (in the fair trade case) material suppliers.[1]

Next to this we have singled out the supply chain (axis 3), to have a more prominent role than in the Bell-Mason diagnostic. Not only may the supply chain be the focus of the venture (as with organic and local food for example) but the supply chain must reflect the values of the venture, and, for so many personal services, must be trusted. In many of the new support services a wide range of trusted specialist suppliers comprise the USC (the 'unique service characteristic') of the service. Their identification and management is the principal innovation.

Diagram 2: Elements for a diagnostic of new social ventures

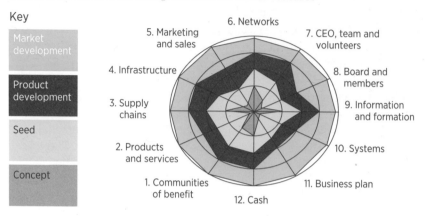

Key

Market development

Product development

Seed

Concept

5. Marketing and sales
6. Networks
7. CEO, team and volunteers
4. Infrastructure
8. Board and members
3. Supply chains
9. Information and formation
2. Products and services
10. Systems
1. Communities of benefit
11. Business plan
12. Cash

We have also included infrastructure and logistics (axis 4) since they relate not only to the supply of the goods of the service, but to their accessibility and to the social interactions that surround them. Small schools, cottage hospitals, local post offices, farmers' markets and village halls all internalise the environmental and social costs of transport and recognise the barriers to access that the centralisation of service points entail. Equally many social and environmental ventures are aimed at more productive use of existing infrastructures – the squatters movement for example, or Landshare, or the out of hours use of school buildings.

We discuss social marketing, financing and business plans separately. Here we identify four other critical axes for social ventures. The first is the principle of extensive social networks (axis 6). These networks are the basis of financial and other forms of support and advice, of volunteer labour and of 'friends in the market'. How to form and sustain these networks is one of the critical issues for successful social venturing.

Second is the importance of looking at the people at the heart of the project, not just at the CEO and the core team, but at a much more extensive group comprising those who contribute time and know-how voluntarily (axis 7). It is one of the characteristics of social projects that they attract support of this kind. How to organise and resource it is one of the key arts of social venturing.

Third, there is the axis of governance (axis 8) and establishing an effective structure of control and support that reflects the purposes of the organisation. In companies limited by guarantee the formal power is with the members, who play a similar role to shareholders, and appoint the Board. This is the formal position. Making it real and effective is another matter and has a whole set of issues when it is a social rather than an economic goal which is the primary driver.

Fourth there is information and formation (axis 9). Bell-Mason's diagnostic was developed for information technology ventures in the late 1980s and early 1990s, prior to the age of the world wide web, and strikingly the issue of information and communications does not have its own axis. Yet the issue is as important as finance because social ventures are by their nature information intensive. Their distinctiveness is often not in the appearance of their product or service, but in its provenance, in the way it is produced, and in the social and environmental issues it addresses. It is about the story and the social connections made through the development of that story.

If one part of the venture then is the chronicling of the story, another is about means of capturing progress (so-called management information systems) to enable the management of all parts of the venture and track its progress. A third is about ensuring there is a system of two-way communications with the wider network, and a fourth a means to stand back and reflect.

These points are further explored in the methods that follow. Here we want to emphasise the value of a diagnostic like that developed by Gordon Bell and Heidi Mason, one that is tailored to the characteristic of the specific venture. We could have suggested double the number of axes, but we favour restricting the number to Bell-Mason's 12 for reasons of practicality.

Bell and Mason take half a day and use 1,000 standard questions along their chosen axes to complete the diagnosis, and feed the results in to expert system software that evaluates the answers based on more than 700 rules and relationships. This then generates a mapping like that shown in the diagram above. There is to our knowledge no comparable diagnostic for social ventures – this would be a useful tool to develop. But in the meantime the axes and the mapping – if adapted along the lines we suggest – do provide a helpful way of preparing and monitoring a new venture.

## Stages

Axes apart, Bell-Mason highlight four stages on any of the chosen axes that are similar to those that we have found useful: the original concept and its development and trialling as a product or service (three stages we have discussed in a separate volume in this series) and the wider launch which is the subject of the present volume. Bell-Mason work towards what they consider a 'steady state', in other words the successful commercialisation of the idea. But in contrast to the launch of a mass commodity or service, we see the launch period of a social venture as a further period of prototyping, with the product idea and business model subject to regular revision and adjustment as its use widens. For social ventures there is rarely a steady state, rather the shaping and reshaping of a cloud.

The value of thinking about the stages is that they raise distinct issues of finance. In Bell-Mason's model (Diagram 3) Stage 1 and 2 are those dealing with the initial development of the idea and are often the hardest to fund. This is certainly the case for social ventures. It might be to explore the concept of making a fair trade shoe – a complex product of 70+ parts and a global industry. Who would finance such a speculative venture, and the follow up of possible leads? Such an initial exploration could throw up some interesting avenues to explore – fair trade rubber for example, or other ethical footwear projects venturing along similar paths (the 'seed' in the Bell-Mason diagram).

Diagram 3: Bell-Mason model

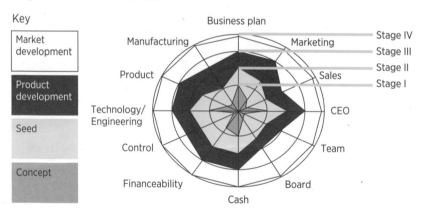

If the avenue proves fruitful there is the product to develop and test, and the supply chain to secure, each requiring larger sums of finance. Finally there is the stage of scaling up for a launch, identifying markets and particularly first users – the first user is often so critical because it allows the venture to show its concept in practice. There are other subsequent stages that we discuss under finance.

What Bell-Mason have done is to map financial needs onto the progress along each of the axes. This allows all those involved in growing and financing the venture to have some perspective on the relative significance of each element of growth. In the words of Bell and Mason, "Falling short on financial goals can be okay in the early stages of a venture, but missing product development milestones is not. In the later stages financial goals become more important. At that point, the venture has to show that it not only has a product but it also has a business. If more than three concepts still need proving the company is engaged in research not product development." A social venture would add its axes to this – but the general point still holds.

Bell and Mason have provided a methodology to analyse the elements involved in successfully launching a private venture. This is also valuable as a tool for social ventures, if other elements such as communities of benefit, social networks, and the formation of the venture's culture are taken into account.

References
www.atamo.com.au/download/BellMasonExplained.pdf

End notes

1  In the case of Divine, it took five years for the union of small cocoa farmers in the Ashanti region of Ghana to form and develop an effective trading capacity on the basis of which a brand could be centred and launched. In many fields that involve marginal producers, fair trade is slow trade.

# 4 ECONOMIC ARCHITECTURE AND BUSINESS PLANS

The process of developing a venture involves a forecast of the future, brought together in a business plan. The business plan will outline an approach – the business model – and detail the preparation of the many elements that go into making a successful venture. But it cannot be a blueprint. It is rather part of the process of the formation of a venture. It is a synthesis of the state of play and a current perspective on the prospects.

This house in Berkeley California was built for Christopher and Stephanie Upham in 1991-2 by the architect Christopher Alexander. He used rough sketch plans rather than detailed drawings, and took decisions progressively in collaboration with the clients, builders, engineers and craftspeople as the house took shape. He called this process 'unfolding'. The house was built on a new type of contract based on a guaranteed price even though the design was not initially fixed. The need to keep to the budget informed the choices made in the course of construction. The architect, who was also the contractor, was paid a normal fixed fee, but spread over a longer period as he was involved in the design and construction process throughout. Alexander called this a 'living process'.

## A new architecture

Christopher Alexander developed his practice and ideas of a living process in opposition to the 'non-living' process that he sees modern construction has become. Each part of the complex sequence of building tends to be designed and built separately without reference to the emerging whole. The architect is a producer of designs at a drawing table, working to specifications laid out by the client. The drawings are checked by an engineer, another engineer works out the foundations, and the construction is undertaken by a contractor overseeing a network of sub contractors. Any changes are difficult and expensive to make. Alexander calls this a mechanised process that, in the 20th century tradition, separates design and execution.

Against this he advocates a different method that cannot be set down in detailed plans drawn up by an architect isolated in a drawing office. Rather each part of a building (as of a town or street) should be treated as a 'living centre' in its own right, and these multiple centres need to be designed and made one by one and adapted each to the other within the whole. The process can still use many of the advances of modern production – whether materials like the new concrete or components like roof tiles – but the oversight of its 'unfolding' remains a collaborative craft process co-ordinated by the architect.

His central proposition that "the nature of order is interwoven in its fundamental character with the nature of the processes which create that order" and that living and liveable buildings have to be made by living processes, draws its inspiration both from the construction processes of the past, and the natural processes elaborated by contemporary complexity theories in physics and biology. His buildings and his books constitute a manifesto for a new architecture.[1]

## Venture architecture

This model of a living process is similar to many of the most successful ventures. Initiatives like Sekem, started with a particular project (**method 18**). In Sekem's case the project was to create an oasis in the desert bio-dynamically.[2] It involved the drilling of wells, the careful design and construction of an appropriate central building and the planting of trees. Soil had to be created through establishing a composting system from which came the first crops. Each of these was a 'living centre', involving its own technologies, designers, suppliers, and manual labourers.

But this was only a beginning. Unlike a building, the process of a venture is never fixed in stone. Its parts continue to grow (or wither). In Sekem, once the core was in place they began to gather particular medicinal herbs, then develop their own herbal teas, which led in turn to the production of herbal medicines. They planted fruit trees and vegetables in their expanding soil, and then organic cotton. This was not Ibrahim Abouleish's original plan. That was more general. Rather it grew in response to particular possibilities (a US importer's request for a herb) or a problem (the contamination of Sekem's organic produce by the spraying of neighbouring cotton crops with pesticide).

This model of organic growth can be found in projects as varied as the Grameen Bank and the Bromley-by-Bow centre, or Twin Trading and Fabio Rosa's pioneering rural electricity in Brazil. In many ways these projects represent the Grameen lending principle. The first loan is small. If the borrower succeeds and the loan is repaid, the next loan can be larger. Operations and finance expand on the basis of what can be achieved and along the paths that have opened up in the course of the work.

On the basis of these and similar projects we can put forward five guiding principles for the start of a venture:

- **Grow step by step**. Just as climbing a mountain involves its base camps, first cols and different routes chosen with an eye to the weather, so in most ventures it is not a matter of moving from prototype to full scale volume production, but rather of finding something that works, with a supply chain and a core team that are reliable. Start-ups will always have something of a second prototype about them, a gamma testing stage following the beta testing. The Italian phrase 'festina lente' is a valuable watchword. Hasten slowly.

- **Flexibility.** Keep the idea firm but the exact methods of realisation open. Divine Chocolate had within four years of its launch in 1998 changed almost all the assumptions on which it had started except for its name and its milk chocolate recipe. The important thing is to have strong feedback and response systems. The Grameen and Danone yoghurt project, which was designed to provide fortified yoghurt to Bangladesh's rural poor, had to switch its business model because the demand from the villages grew too slowly. In spite of initial prototyping and market testing of different yoghurts, when the larger scale production came on stream the prices turned out to be too high and the product too unusual for many villagers. So the project changed course, and switched to selling to the urban middle class. The aim was to generate enough volume and profit, so that the business could return to the rural poor with a cheaper and established product.[3]

- **Small cells for big systems.** There will always be a leap from prototype to volume, but the leap can be narrowed by searching out (or developing) micro technologies and micro markets. Cafédirect started by selling Roast and Ground coffee (low volume production runs to be sold through high margin ethical outlets) before moving to the higher volume Freeze Dried that had to be sold through supermarkets. The stakes were less for Roast and Ground, and production runs could be more easily adjusted. On similar principles, the London Borough of Haringey's recycling scheme grew step by step by using small electric controlled vehicles that ran on the pavement and were one tenth of the cost of a conventional waste truck. The initial coverage could be small and investments less.

- **The corset of cost.** For new ventures supplying to contract (such as social services for the state) revenue will be secure, with uncertainty centred on the ability to provide the contracted service within the targeted cost. For those selling into a market, it is costs that can be controlled and markets that are uncertain. For many social enterprises the question will be what can be delivered by an operation with an overhead of say £0.5 million. In such cases the aim should be to limit the 'income leap' – that gap between overhead and income that has to be funded by initial capital – by observing a corset of cost. Impatient growth makes the future fragile.

- **Capital sufficiency.** Initial capital funds the leap between costs and income (the cost of the build up). It is an insurance (reserve) against falling short. Many ventures flounder because the leap is too great and capital inadequate. The tortoise requires less initial finance than the hare and stretches it out longer. Slow growth requires slow finance.

No venture can be created without risk and danger. As with all art, social venturing requires creators rather than auditors, risk lovers not risk averters. These principles – to hasten slowly and preserve flexibility – are based not on a fear of risk but a recognition of what is involved in developing a venture as a living process. Not to do so will increase the risk. To do so will increase the chance of economic sustainability and keeping within the budget.

There will always be pressures to quicken the pace. For social ventures it is above all the urgency of the need. But other factors often come into play like the narrow window of first mover advantage for an innovative social enterprise, or the impatience that marks all idealism of realising the idea in practice. Yet if it is to remain a living process then it takes time. Relational capital grows slowly. Craft takes longer than standardised production. To build the Uphams' house took longer than the norm. Fair trade chains take at least five years to grow, and brands another seven. But the result is that the roots are deep and the venture more resilient.

## Business Plans

A business plan should not be developed like detailed architects' drawings that specify a future that it is the task of the staff to deliver. It should perform a different set of functions:

• it sets out the idea behind the venture and its business model, and provides a first sketch of how this will be realised

• it lays out an operational agenda and demonstrates the extent to which the venture's creators have considered and prepared the many elements that will go into the venture's operation – all those items in the social Bell-Mason diagram

• it specifies the financial parameters of the venture and provides one or more financial forecasts

• it demonstrates the financial modelling capacity already in the venture

• it provides an inventory of all types of capital in place and required – financial capital, human capital and relational capital

• it is a base case that can then be amended and supplemented as the venture proceeds

• it is a core document for developing a common perspective among all those involved in the venture both in terms of goals and the means of realising them. It is a chart of the operational territory and the desired destinations. It is not just a technical document to convince those who are approached to finance it. It is a social document that integrates the venture.

Business plans should reflect in their goals, their scope and their process the values that the venture seeks to realise. They are the basis for what all social ventures rely on – for their finance and practical support – the material basis of hope.

Social venturing is not the implementation of a blueprint but a process of unfolding. Each of the many elements that are necessary for the operation of a successful venture should be treated as 'living centres' designed to embody the spirit of the venture with an eye to their integration in the productive system as a whole. Business Plans cannot design the future. Rather they provide a chart of the venture's theatre of operations and demonstrate the competence of those engaged to take the venture forward.

End notes

1  Of his many works see in particular volumes 2 and 3 of The Nature of Order, The Centre for Environmental Structure, 2002, (the description of the process of making the Uphams' house is contained in an Appendix to Volume 2) and also the remarkable, A Pattern Language (with Sara Ishikawa and Murray Silverstein), Oxford University Press, 1977. On large projects, something of this integration is being achieved through the application of Toyota's methods to construction. The Integrated Project Delivery model seeks to combine the open-endedness advocated by Alexander, with the discipline of cost and schedule. By introducing a methodology based on a fully integrated team of designer, contractor, client, cost estimator etc. buildings of great complexity can be built with the critical decisions being made sequentially and incrementally within an agreed framework of principles. See also the approach and work of the French architect Jean Nouvel, www.jeannouvel.com.

2  For this remarkable story, that exemplifies Christopher Alexander's method in developing a sustainable community in the middle of the Egyptian desert, see Ibrahim Abouleish, Sekem, Floris Books, 2005.

3  The story of the Grameen-Danone yoghurt partnership illustrates the value of a social project being able to draw on the technical and innovative capacity of a large corporation willing to work on the social project's terms. It is told by Muhammad Yunus in chapter 4 and 5 of Creating a World Without Poverty: Social Business and the Future of Capitalism, Public Affairs 2008. For an update see Liam Black, "Pots of Gold" The Guardian, 17th February 2009.

# 5 SETTING UP THE VENTURE

There comes a point when every venture has to decide what organisational form to take, what kind of decision-making process to adopt and which kinds of information and financial management systems to put in place. These decisions can be costly and time consuming. But getting it right early on provides structures and systems which act as skeletons that help hold the organisation together.

Un Techo Para Chile (A Roof for Chile) was set up in 1997 to provide decent housing for some of Chile's poorest citizens. Under the programme, recent graduates and young professionals spend two years working on various projects, building houses and turning slum dwellings into safe and decent homes (as pictured above). The organisation has now spread across South America, enlisting hundreds of thousands of volunteers to build over 40,000 homes. By 2010, they hope to build a further 10,000 homes across the continent.

Until 2005 Un Techo Para Chile had no legal status – it was simply a loose network of students, young professionals and residents. Felipe Berrios who launched the initiative believed that this was the best arrangement – it allowed the volunteers to have ownership over the project and also meant that Un Techo Para Chile could not be sued by landowners. In 2005, Un Techo Para Chile began to collaborate and work with the government to provide housing on government land. In order to do so, they had to become legally constituted.

Once you have an idea – and some support – the next stage is to get the thing up and running. This means getting processes and structures in place. This can be fluid and informal as in the case of Un Techo Para Chile. But to receive significant grants or to contract with the state projects need to become legal entities.

There are numerous organisational forms – Community Interest Companies, Companies Limited by Guarantee, Industrial and Provident Societies and so on (see **methods 7-10**). The form chosen has ramifications for accountability, auditing, finance and governance that are usually laid out in the governing documents. These documents – constitutions, mission statements, memoranda of association, articles of association, trust deeds and so on – outline the objects of the organisation and how it will be administered, managed and governed (such as the process and criteria for appointing directors and trustees). So, depending on the organisational form selected, the next task is to identify, select (and persuade) supporters to become members of the board or trustees.

There is a value in thinking through appropriate legal and governance forms together rather than leaving it to one or two people in consultation with lawyers. For it is a means of reaching a common understanding on the purpose of the venture and the principles on which it wishes to operate. This clarity gives strength to the skeleton, which can otherwise remain brittle.

But there are two issues to note. First these structures can set a mould that suits one stage but not another, and it may be practically costly and time consuming to change them. So it is useful to build in flexibility from the start and periodically review these structures as part of the venture's reflective processes (**method 20**). For example, it is difficult to have user representatives before there are users, but the shell of a structure can be put in place that can be filled in due course. Thus the Lyndoch EcoVillage (**method 2**) started with a small development board with a view to establishing a house owner controlled entity which the Board could contract to run the village once the houses were built.

Secondly, the establishment process takes time and money. In some cases, the costs of seeking legal advice can be prohibitive for social ventures, and has certainly been one of the factors in limiting the use of Limited Liability Partnerships (**method 9**). One organisation that is currently working on a way to reduce these costs is One Click Organisations. It is a new web platform that enables informal groups to create simple legal structures and make collective decisions. The platform is intended to help social enterprises, collectives, activist groups and other kinds of associations, by removing some of the barriers these groups face in writing up constitutions and becoming legal entities.

The idea is that a group organiser would go to the website, answer a series of questions about the group's objectives, how decisions are made and how people can get involved. With this information, a constitution and dedicated company website is automatically generated, and emails are sent out to founding members with details of the founding meeting. A legal entity linked to the One Click platform is then created at the founding meeting.

As the platform develops more options will become available – including a company limited by guarantee, limited liability partnerships, company limited by shares and so on. Hopefully, they will develop peer to peer forums where new projects can receive advice, and economic means for a specialist to review the draft documents drawn up from this process. As we are learning with all such sites, active hosting can greatly increase their value.

Yet even as it stands, One Click Organisations is the first project to our knowledge that links legal constitutions with electronic information systems. It promises to radically reduce the costs associated with devising a constitution, becoming a legal entity and adopting participatory forms of decision-making.

Similar services would greatly aid the introduction of other elements of the venture's systems. There are already platforms such as wordpress.org. that provide free programmes for establishing and managing a website, including wikis and chat rooms. It would be valuable to develop similar services for drawing up social business plans, and putting in place financial management processes, and management information systems. The idea would be to create a platform that could provide all the back office functions needed when setting up, for it is one of the disadvantages for new ventures that they are forced to adopt and operate systems of their own when it would be more economic to share them.

From our experience new ventures are understandably reluctant to contract out these backroom services, but often lack the resources to develop adequate systems of their own. A means of sharing knowledge and systems between social ventures on a plug and pay basis promises not only to improve operations but free up resources.

New ventures often incur substantial start-up costs yet economise on systems. What is needed are means for social ventures to access free legal and system programmes and know-how – building on the promising initiative of One Click Organisations.

Link
One Click Organisations http://www.oneclickor.gs/

# SECTION 2:
# OWNERSHIP AND GOVERNANCE

Mission-driven organisations face three issues in deciding on a suitable organisational form:

- the mission and what it will take to realise it

- ownership and how this is translated into governance

- access to finance which re-enforces the mission

Within the public sector these issues are clear. Ultimately the mission comes from elected representatives. Ownership lies with the state, as mediated by its departments and agencies. Finance comes from tax. With a private market corporation these issues are equally clear. The primary purpose is the maximisation of financial returns. Ownership and the forms of finance determine the extent of the claims on the profits produced. There is a continuum between those with least security and the greatest formal say over operations and the resultant profits, running through to those with greater security, specified returns (a rate of interest) and little say in the governance of the company. The overall goals are shared, and ownership confers rights of organisational control and financial distribution.

In the social economy the issues are not so easily pinned down. The mission motive is less precise than the profit motive. Success in realising it cannot be distributed like a dividend. Ownership needs to reflect the mission and involve those who need to share in decisions about the direction and operations of the organisation. It is no longer at root a financial concept but a mobilising one, indeed those providing finance may have interests at odds with the mission.

Many of the tensions in the social economy are the result of a lack of clarity on these issues. The legal forms may address one problem (democratic governance) but not another (how equity finance can be raised). The mission may be so general that it fails to integrate the board, the staff, and the beneficiaries at the level of practice. Within a social organisation there is commonly a continuing triangular tension between governance, the social beneficiaries, and finance. The art is how to get all three in line.

# 6 OWNERSHIP

In the social economy ownership is an ambiguous concept. Its organisational structures are the site of contending pressures of goals and interests. The organisation may have a social goal of benefitting others, but to do so it involves those with some measure of private interests – finance, staff, suppliers and purchasers. Some may exercise their interests at arms length – and their market or financial power may be such as to reduce the social project to little more than a sub-contractor or agent, severely restricting the autonomy of the owners. But others may seek closer involvement in the project's direction. How can the forms of ownership and governance accommodate these pressures and turn them to good account?

Co-operative drinking. To save their local pub, 125 villagers in Hesket Newmarket in Cumbria (shown above on the village green outside the pub) formed a co-op and bought it. Two years previously they had formed another co-op to buy the micro brewery attached to it. Dividends are paid in pints rather than pounds. The brewery is one of 24 micro breweries in Cumbria, and 383 in the UK, almost all established in the past 30 years. There has been a similar growth in North America (micro breweries in the US went from eight to 1,492 between 1980 and 2003), part of brewing's own micro revolution. Most are family run, but Hesket Newmarket is the pioneer of a drinkers' co-operative.

From one perspective, the form of ownership – whose details tend to be dry and complex – are in effect a set of rules about who has the right to decide on the mission, on how an asset is used and how its yield is distributed. They are rules about goals, governance and distribution. They define a space within which negotiations take place and decisions are made about the direction and conduct of the organisation. They act as a container – a holding structure – for differences and their resolution.

From another perspective ownership is part of a social project's means of mobilisation, of encouraging a sense in others that the project is theirs. This may be in the tangible form of a share. But it is the reality of the share that matters – whether it gives the holder of the share a sense of involvement in the project's decision making, as well as a stake in its financial success. The form of ownership is the skeleton, but it is made flesh through the qualitative processes that take place within that form.

## Associate or combine

There are two main forms of social organisation, associations and combinations. In associations all owners form a single class and have equal rights within that class. They operate on the principle of one person one vote, irrespective of the finance and time they contribute. Combinations are assemblies of difference – different interests, different contributions and different degrees of commitment.

## Associations

Associations include clubs, partnerships, and a wide range of co-operatives, mutual insurance companies, and friendly societies (see **method 7**). They also include companies limited by guarantee, the UK form of not for profits, where there are no formal shareholders or 'owners' but rather members who elect a governing Board. Social enterprises, NGOs like Oxfam, student unions, sports associations like the European golf tour or the England and Wales Cricket Board, and even the UK's railways (Network Rail) take this form.

These associations have one or more limitations. The first is a limitation of finance. These companies find it difficult to raise equity – co-ops because the voting power of shares is distributed equally among members irrespective of their financial contributions, and companies limited by guarantee because they have no shares to offer.

The second is a limitation in governance. Those social companies which are set up to benefit others, customarily take on charitable status which entails the adoption of a sharp and limiting distinction between donors and beneficiaries. While in co-ops the beneficiaries are placed at the centre of governance, in charities they are excluded, for it is inherent in the concept of charity that the beneficiaries should not be involved in governance or in any form of charitable ownership.

The roots of this restriction run deep. The concept of charity developed side by side with capitalism from the late 16th century – it was for the rich to help the poor. There were two separate categories – the donor (active) and the receiver (passive) connected by the act of giving. This binary relationship is parallel to that of the seller and the buyer in a market economy connected by the act of exchange. Charities could not have the receiver taking part in the act of giving without disrupting this distinction. The principle is a foundation stone of UK charity law which specifies that the beneficiaries may not be part of the governance structure of a charity.

The third limitation is one on activity. The concept of charity is that it is about giving not trade. As a result it is common for social projects to have a dual structure, a trading arm operating in the market and a charitable wing funded by grants engaged in activities like education, advice and providing information. The Charity Commission goes to some length to keep these separate, by encouraging distinct boards, and the careful allocation of staff time between the two companies.

The restrictions imposed by charitable status – a status that in effect provides a government sanctioned grant in the form of tax exemption on charitable donations – are coming under strain. For it is clear that much social trading has an equivalent purpose to charities. It is also important for grant funded organisations to be able to trade, and for the beneficiaries of these initiatives to be included in their ownership and governance. Recently there has been a growing recognition of these issues by the Charity Commission, though as yet no formal change in the legal status of charities and the long-standing concept underlying it.

## Combinations

The alternative to associations is combinations. They are social companies that wish to raise equity and accommodate different interests in their ownership and governance structures. Some have opted for conventional company forms in which voting power reflects the quantity of common shares held, and boards represent the main interests involved. In this sense the conventional company structure is more open and flexible. But it too has its dangers, in that it lacks the explicit protection of the mission and its beneficiaries contained in co-ops and charities.

In 2005 the UK government introduced a new company status to rectify the potential dangers of using conventional company forms for social purposes. Companies could retain their various traditional forms (as co-ops, or companies limited by guarantees or ordinary limited companies) but they could register as Community Interest Companies (CIC). Although CICs do not qualify for charitable tax relief directly, recently a way has been found for charities to invest in the equity of a CIC, which is a major step forward (**method 8**).

## Hybrids

In the end these company structures and legal statuses are merely shells. They can help defend the primacy of the mission, but they can be diverted by other interests – by the managers of co-ops or not for profit companies and their level of payment for example. At the same time they can be moulded to common goals. For example co-ops are considering how to take other stakeholders into account in their governance. Companies limited by guarantee can have different classes of membership each with their own rights. The constitutions of conventional trading companies together with shareholder agreements can specify a governance structure in which the mission remains primary.

## Underlying principles

What is important therefore is to be clear about the principles to be reflected in the company's ownership and governance. We suggest eight:

1.  the financial imperative should be subordinate to the social one

2.  there should be structures whose task is to develop and diffuse the social purpose and principles of the enterprise

3.  finance should be structured so that the beneficiaries have a principal claim on dividends and capital appreciation

4.  the primary beneficiaries and/or their representatives should be engaged in the ownership and control of the project

5.  ownership and governance entail learning and education

6.  ownership is part of a wider strategy of mobilisation

7.  ownership should be thought of as an experience not merely a set of legal rights, and should be organised accordingly

8.  safeguards should be built in from the beginning to protect projects from their own success (either from takeover or destruction by those threatened by the success)

For each of these there are methods. Some are discussed in what follows in terms of organisational forms, and financing instruments and strategies. The co-operative movement has given particular attention to these issues, aware as it is that its principles of organisation are more than economic instruments but rather embody a social ethic. Their positive (and negative) lessons need to be spread and adapted within the social economy as a whole.

Lawyers are the builders of constitutions, but the social innovators should be the architects. They should set down the principles that they want to see reflected in the organisational structure and provisions of governance, and find ways of ensuring that the social imperative of the project remains the dominant one. We approach ownership in terms of empowerment, fitness, mobilisation, learning, experience and the distribution of benefits. Each of these requires its own version of social innovation.

# 7 CO-OPS AND ASSOCIATIONS

Co-ops, associations, clubs, mutual insurance companies and friendly societies all have an associative form. These forms – many of which have a long history – are adopted where mutuality and equality are paramount. Their defining purpose is the interests of their members. But their culture is social, committed to the communities in which they operate, providing work, services, and support. The formal beneficiaries of the co-op are the owners, and they resolve the tension between social and financial goals by structurally subordinating the latter.

Of Europe's largest worker co-operatives, the oldest is the Ceramic Co-operative of Imola in the Emilia Romagna region of Italy. The factory was transferred to worker ownership by its founder in 1874 on the basis of the republican principles of its founder. It is now the largest ceramic tile producer in Europe, with a turnover of €400 million, 70 per cent of it exports, with 1,500 employees and seven factories. At the core of the co-op are 170 skilled workers who meet monthly to discuss operations with the management (most of whom are not members of the co-op) and make decisions. Members have to be between the ages of 25 and 40 to join, and pay €100,000 which they can borrow from the co-op and pay back from their share of dividends. There is no capital appreciation, so they receive back their €100,000 when they leave. As of 2004, 12 per cent of the co-op members were women, one of whom was on the seven person Board.

## A co-operative civil economy

In the UK co-operatives stretch back to artisan co-ops of the early 19th century and the consumer co-ops of the 1840s (Rochdale Pioneers started in 1844). The 19th century mutual economy centred on co-operative shops, farms, workshops, banks, insurance companies and friendly societies. By the end of the century 80 per cent of men of working age were members of one or more friendly society (90 per cent in Australia).

While it never developed into an autonomous economy as some of its leaders once hoped, it has survived and has been growing in the early years of the 21st century. There are currently 4,500 co-ops in the UK, with a turnover of £26.3 billion, largely accounted for by the 80 largest co-ops. 400 of them are workers' co-ops, the largest being Suma Wholefoods with a turnover of £24 million. There are 420 Friendly Societies, 750 credit unions, 1,700 working men's club and 60 building societies.

## The continental European tradition

Elsewhere in Europe there are regions where co-ops have developed semi autonomous economies. Emilia Romagna is one of a number of Italian regions where co-operatives have been the basis of a resilient industrial expansion. Farmers' co-ops have sold to co-operative processors (often farmer owned) who have developed co-operative brands and marks (Parmesan cheese for example) and have then sold to co-operative wholesalers and retailers. They have borrowed from co-operative banks, and covered their risks through co-operative insurance companies. There are now over 8,000 co-ops operating in Emilia Romagna, some of which are the dominant firms in Europe in their particular sector. Of the 25 largest workers co-ops in Europe in 2008, half were in Emilia Romagna.[1]

What marks out these Italian regions, however, is that they have developed a complex structure of co-operation between firms. The firms form consortia for specific purposes, to promote overseas sales for example, or sourcing the latest technology, or providing mutual finance. For the smallest firms, the National Confederation of Artisans (CNA) takes on many of the overhead functions of accounting, invoicing, reporting as well as representing the interests of small artisans in Rome.[2]

## Producer co-ops in the South

Anyone who has visited the co-ops of Emilia Romagna, or Tuscany, Umbria, La Marche and similar regions in Spain will recognise that producer co ops are a living not a dying form. The same is true of the multiplicity of producer co-ops in the developing world that form the bedrock of the fair trade movement. In the latter case, the agricultural co-ops in Africa had grown rapidly in the 1960s and 1970s – often promoted by governments as a form of economic democracy – but by the 1990s had often become too large, bureaucratic and in some cases corrupt. Fair trade has provided a secure market and organisational support that has allowed these older co-ops to restructure themselves, and has created the conditions for new ones to be formed. Kuapa Kokoo in Ghana, for example, formed in 1993 as an association of 1,000 farmers, now has 45,000 members organised in over 1,200 villages societies and has become one of the major cocoa traders in Ghana as a result.

There is a parallel story in Asia and in Central and South America. In the latter co-ops had been weakened by neo-liberal policies, but have had a resurgence thanks in part to the expansion of fair trade markets. To take only one example out of many, in the South West of Costa Rica, when Chiquita decided to close its banana plantations in the region in 1980, the workers in one plantation negotiated to take over the land and packing plant as a producer co-op, Coopetrabasur. It sold its bananas for a fixed period to Chiquita and from the mid 1990s to the Dutch based fair trade company Agrofair, of which it had a share of the equity. Again, all those who make the long journey over the mountains to this outby region of Costa Rica will recognise that the co-operative form is a living, operational structure, embedded in its local community in which it plays the role of the primary source of wealth and employment.

## Service co-ops

There is also a strong tradition of service co-ops – not just in the retail sector where co-ops have dominated in Scandinavia and Switzerland – but in housing and most recently in social services, health and education. Italian social co-ops now number 7,000 with a turnover of €5 billion and combine providers, volunteers and recipients of social services (type A) as well as permanent workers and those wanting to enter the workforce – particularly disadvantaged groups (type B). The social and housing co-ops (notably those in Canada) have as one of their driving principles the integration of marginal social groups as service beneficiaries and as service providers, supplying the education and training to enable them to fulfil one of the oldest co-operative tenets of self responsibility (see **method 20**).

## Nine considerations

From this range of examples of flourishing co-operatives, we identify nine issues for social innovators to consider when considering suitable forms for their start-ups:

i) Co-ops work best where they bring together comparable people or organisations, which have their own autonomous yet common identity, as farmers, or skilled workers, consumers, residents, or in the Italian case small firms.

ii) Co-ops exist primarily to serve the interests of their members, and this puts people at the centre of their organisational culture. Education has therefore always been a leading theme in co-operatives from the Rochdale pioneers onwards, particularly geared to their capacity to play the role of active members, with the skills of collaboration, and the understanding of the principle and practice of mutualism.

iii) The tension between workers and management in workers co-ops is not dissolved by the workers becoming their own managers (except in small co-ops) but by making managers responsible to workers. The traditional hierarchy of ownership/board/management/workers is turned on its head when the workers becomes the owners and nominate the board.

iv) A further tension in co-ops is between the nature of the production process and the democratic apparatus. Some of the large agricultural and consumer co-ops modelled themselves on unsophisticated versions of mass production and distribution, with a strict division between managerial and unskilled labour. It was then culturally and technically difficult for the unskilled workers to have effective control over the executive (since they had none of the know-how) or to be committed to an organisation offering limited work satisfaction. Some co-ops have sought ways round this by circulating skilled and unskilled jobs, while others have consciously adopted more human centred production methods and technologies.

v) Worker co-ops have defined their boundaries in terms of commitment, skill, financial contribution, ownership of assets, and length of service. This has created a division in many worker co-ops between the co-op members and those employees not in the co-op. Coopetrabasur in Costa Rica has a ratio of two non members to one member, and in this case the non members have formed their own service co-op, Coopsersur, which negotiates terms and conditions with the agricultural co-op and participates in the decisions on the allocation of the fair trade premium.

vi) Co-operative ownership is a way of gaining the loyalty and commitment of the workforce which is critical in the knowledge economy where the skill and knowledge of workers is the key asset of the enterprise. One of the reasons for the success of the Co-operative Ceramica d'Imola is that the core of the skilled workers has remained in the firm over the long term.

vii) Co-operatives also encourage a long term perspective in the enterprise, by their measure of protection from takeovers for short term financial reasons. There was a push to demutualise a number of British building societies in the 1980s and 1990s by offering substantial sums to the mainly consumer members, but the recent financial crisis has shown this to have been a disastrous move, and has left those societies who remained mutual remarkably healthy.

viii) For consumer or investor co-ops a critical issue is how to ensure that members feel a real sense of ownership of the organisation. If the consumers are regulars (as in The Old Crown Pub, **method 6**) this is less of a problem, but when they are dispersed the organisers need to think of ways in which their members can contribute to and experience the work of the co-operative and not merely become passive recipients of a dividend (see for example Ebbsfleet United, **method 15**).

ix) The principle of one member one vote, as found in co-ops, insulates this form of democratic governance from the influence of finance, but in doing so they reduce its supply. Co-ops have had to rely on equity contributed by their own members, on re-invested earnings, and loans.

Co-ops like all firms go through periods of crisis, but the co-operative structure is sufficiently robust to allow restructuring to take place without the breakup of the organisation and the forced sale of its components. Co-ops are a remarkably resilient form of mutual form of economic organisation, which have proved adaptable to many different areas of the economy. They have tended to grow and contract in cycles – and have been strongest in periods and areas where there is a strong sense of social cohesion and commitment to reciprocity within and beyond the organisation. The democratic and human centred principles of 19th century co-operation have been a constant unifying theme, and have provided a clear set of social principles to govern the conduct and processes of both producer and consumer co-ops.

End notes

1   European Federation of Employee Share Ownership, The European Employee Ownership top 100 2008.

2   An excellent account of the complex institutional web of the so-called Third Italy is in Chapters 7 and 8 of Michael Best, The New Competition, Polity Press, 1990.

# 8 COMMUNITY INTEREST COMPANIES

The strict demarcation between charities whose aim is to benefit others, and private companies whose interest is to benefit their shareholders has become problematic. It has meant that charities have been limited in their sources of funds, in their scope as traders and the involvement of their beneficiaries. The culture has been that of service rather than enterprise. How do you have a form of organisation that bridges both?

The opening procession of the 2008 annual assembly of Liberation Nuts and the International Nut Producer Co-operative (INPC) in Kelakam, India. Liberation Nuts is a UK Community Interest Company, owned by nut producers (42 per cent) fair trade companies (35 per cent) and ethical investors (23 per cent). The nut producer share is owned by the INPC, an international co-operative with members from 11 nut producer co-operatives, located in the Amazon region, Central America, southern Africa and Kerala, India. The INPC annual assembly is held at the same time as the Liberation Annual assembly and circulates among the countries of the co-operatives involved. The aim of the assemblies is not merely to make decisions about the current and future directions of the organisations, but to make ownership and people-to-people trade 'real' for all those involved.

Social enterprises, or hybrids that seek to involve private as well as public and social investors, should consider adopting a Community of Interest Company (CIC) status for their enterprise. This is equivalent to the status of a charity in that the company has an overriding social or environmental goal, but it is more flexible in that it allows the investors to earn a return without the drive for financial returns taking over. It allows the top line to remain in control over the bottom line. And in its latest development, it allows charities to invest in the equity of a CIC, opening up a whole new source of equity funding.

## Protecting the mission

CICs were established under the Community Interest Act of 2004 and the Regulations of 2005, explicitly to reduce the tension between social goals and external finance. The CIC can take any existing company form but with CIC status.

The way in which this new status addresses the tension between finance and mission is by making the mission dominant and limiting returns on capital. The articles of CIC companies have the 'communities of benefit' as their primary rationale, and each year a CIC has to file a return with the CIC regulator showing its impact on the 'community of benefit'.

Equity holders can make a return but this is limited in three ways:

• a limit of aggregate dividends to 35 per cent of profits

• a limit of the amount of the dividend per share (currently the maximum dividend is 5 per cent over the Bank of England base rate)

• an asset lock, which prescribes that asset sale must be at market value, or transferred to another CIC or charity, so that any increase in value is retained for the benefit of 'the community of interest'.

The aim of these provisions is to create a protected economy where the social goal remains dominant. Dividends and asset sales can be made without restrictions to other CICs or charities, but not to private investors. For investors, there is a modest rate of return, and it is assumed that this will be reflected in a stable value of shares.

Any investor is free to sell their shares, but because of the dividend lock they are assumed to be unlikely to have significant (or indeed any) capital gain. These restrictions thus dampen the normal drive of capital to maximise its returns. The CIC regulator (charged with administering the CIC protected 'social economy') refers to the need to ensure that windfall profits (and by implication increased asset values) are returned to the benefit of the community.

The CIC form has been criticised on the grounds that its rates of return do not reflect risk, and that CICs are therefore unattractive to venture capital. But again this is to look at the issue through the lens of conventional finance, for CICs have attracted funds from those willing to risk their capital because of the social returns.

## The growth of CICs

As of June 2009, 2,816 companies in the UK had registered as CICs, over 80 per cent of which were in real estate and various services (health, education, social and personal services). A typical sample includes a fostercare service, a theatre, youth enterprises, craftworks, an environmental project as well as Liberation Nuts, the fair trade nut company shown in the picture on page 69.

In the case of Liberation Nuts, after the proof of concept phase, funded by the Alternative Trading Organisations (ATOs) involved, its start-up was financed by venture philanthropists and a Dutch ethical bank with close links to a development agency. But during this financing process, the company discovered a new source of venture finance – mission oriented charities – that the CIC regulator and the Charities Aid Foundation agreed could invest in the equity of a CIC.

This venture charity finance was entirely consistent with the company's social goals. From the investing charity's point of view, a venture might be risky, but any return would be greater than if it had simply gifted the money. Since the social goals of a CIC are similar in kind to those of a charity, the CIC opened up the possibility of charities entering the market, and of overcoming the traditional split between donors and receivers by partnering with 'communities of benefit'.

The principal of alignment between core finance and the social goals of the enterprise we refer to as 'the Liberation Principle'. From this perspective, CICs have been an important innovation for the expansion of the social economy.

Community of Interest Companies are an innovative form of social company whose aim is to allow social ventures to access equity investment while maintaining the social goals of the enterprise as paramount. They do this through having a cap on dividends, which insulates the enterprise from the private market's imperative for profit maximisation and capital growth. While it may discourage some private risk investors seeking higher returns, in practice there have been investors who have in effect taken on this risk premium as their contribution to the social investment.

References

www.cicregulator.gov.uk

Sid Gould, Social Enterprise and Business Structures in Canada, Fraser Valley Centre for Social Enterprise February 2006

# 9 STAKEHOLDER GOVERNANCE

Associations and co-ops are assumed to have a common interest, with clearly demarcated characteristics of a member: consumer, producer, resident, or investor. Many projects have more than one constituency that they are designed to benefit, or whose commitment the project wants to secure. Can such different interests be included in project governance without compromising the main social purpose or weighing down operations with unproductive wrangling?

A tree nursery in a forest certified by the Forestry Stewardship Council (FSC). The FSC was established in 1992 to establish good practice in the maintenance and harvesting of timber. It brought together environmentalists, indigenous people's organisations, community forestry groups, and environmentally concerned forestry professions, timber traders and forestry companies. By 2008 it had issued 7,500 certificates covering seven per cent of the world's forest and 40 per cent of the companies in the forestry supply chain. The value of FSC labeled sales to date is $20 billion.

Given the differing interests, the FSC developed a tripartite structure of governance. There are three chambers, Environmental, Social and Economic, all of which can have unlimited numbers of members. To ensure equal geographic representation each of these chambers in turn comprises north and south sub-chambers with unlimited membership that have equal voting rights within their chambers.

To maintain the balance of voting power between different interests . each of the three chambers elect three members onto a nine person board, and all decisions require a majority from each of the three groups to be approved. Any two people from one chamber therefore have effective veto power. As with all constitutions designed to protect minority interests (such as the Northern Ireland Assembly) this encourages compromise without any one individual having the power to block decision making.

The integration of different interests around a common purpose cannot be achieved through project constitutions alone. But constitutions and formal agreements can help in providing incentives to reach agreement, and safeguarding voices that might otherwise get lost.

There are three ways in which different interests can be taken into account:

*   By adopting formal structures which embed the different interests in the constitutional concept

*   By having different classes of membership or shares, with particular rights attached to each

*   By adopting a form of 'open capital' or 'open corporate partnership' through which all parties with an interest in the success of a project can participate in its governance and its financial return

## Collegiate government

A venture can establish a formal colleges of members – as the Forestry Stewardship Council has done – with equal rights in governance, and provisions safeguarding minorities. This has the virtue of clarity and explicitness. Its limitations are its inflexibility with respect to changes in the relative significance of the different parties, and in the case of enterprises, variations in financial contributions.

## Classes of membership

Any general corporate form – whether co-op or company – can include in its constitution or through a shareholders agreement, provisions giving particular rights to a class of members or indeed to particular shareholders. For example in the fair trade fruit company Agrofair, the northern partners held A shares, and the producer co-operatives B shares, and each had the right to nominate one member to a three person Board. Constitutional and other major decisions required the agreement of both parties, including decisions on those fruit suppliers who were admitted to CPAF, the international producers co-op, that held the B shares.

In the fair trade nut company Liberation, there are three categories of shareholders: alternative trading organisations, the international producer co-op, and ethical investors. Each has the right to nominate a specified number of people to the Board, while voting as shareholders according to their number of shares.

## Open corporate partnerships

A third alternative, the Limited Liability Partnership, is still in its infancy in the social economy. LLPs came into effect in the UK in 2001 in order to limit the liability of partners in accountancy and similar professional practices. The LLP is a legal entity that can own property, employ people and enter into contracts, and is responsible for its debts as with a limited company.

The LLP is, however, much more flexible than a company or co-op. It is governed by an LLP Agreement. This specifies how the partnership is managed, how profits are divided, capital invested, disputes resolved, exits organised and so on. There is no defined structure and these agreements can be easily amended. Although the form was originally introduced for private partnerships, it is equally suited to social enterprises or co-operatives – the principles of each being laid down in the partnership agreement.

This new form has been called an 'open corporate partnership'. It paves the way for a new concept of 'open capital'. For it allows any stakeholders – 'beneficiaries', staff, suppliers, financiers – to become a partner and share a common interest in the success of the firm. A number of technology start-ups have used an LLP for this reason. Start-ups are risky and the LLP involves all stakeholders in both the risk and reward of the start-up – aligning their interests in success.

An early corporate example is the Hilton Hotels. They sold a portfolio of 10 hotels in 2002 for £350 million to an LLP in which Hilton owned 40 per cent, with the other 60 per cent being owned by another LLP linking 3 investor members including the Bank of Scotland. Under the LLP agreement the investor LLP received 28.8 per cent of the gross revenues from the hotels for 27 years, plus a further £3m annually.

The investor stake was a form of temporary equity (in contrast say to the money being advanced as a loan secured by a mortgage, or a sale and leaseback). This avoided an overhead of interest or rental charges, and gave the investors more security than they would have received through a traditional equity stake. Crucially it aligned the interests of those who would otherwise have been adversaries, the one as borrower, the other as lender.

The social economy has yet to take full advantage of this new form. A workers co-op called 2amase was established as an LLP in 2004, to provide training and consultancy to other social enterprises. The rationale was that it allowed them to introduce new members easily, and to remain self employed. The Hub (a social enterprise providing office space for other social enterprises) adopted the LLP form, but found that it was still little known in the legal profession and as a result the legal fees involved outweighed the benefits. Yet experience is growing in the social sector through lawyers being involved directly in projects and a current project to develop a low carbon car (see **method 19**) is being developed as an LLP because of the risk and reward benefits involved.

Once it becomes better known, the form would also allow a co-op (or any social enterprise) to raise capital, giving investors a stake in the success of the operation for a given period of time (as with the Hilton investors) without compromising the co-operative principle.

There are other occasions when the flexibility of the LLP could be appropriate: the purchase and operations of a community land trust for example, or the establishment of a solar array or community owned windmill. There has also been considerable interest in LLPs from the Muslim world because – in creating a continuity between capital as a static value and money as operationally dynamic – it dissolves the traditional categories of equity and debt.

The value of considering different stakeholder interests from the beginning is that it helps to clarify the central purpose of the social project, those for whom the project is being established, what coalitions are needed to take it forward, which of these interests are consistent with the philosophy and culture of the project and therefore appropriate to be included in the core governance of the organisation. Once these points are clear there are a range of ways in which those core stakeholders can be incorporated in the structure of the organisation and its processes – through the venture's constitution, 'a shareholders' agreement' or the terms of a limited partnership.

References

Chris Cook. Open Capital. If Not Global Capitalism Then What? Paper presented to the Centre for the Study of Global Ethics- University of Birmingham, October 2003 http://www.opencapital.net/papers/ifnotglobal.htm

Links

www.fsc.org/governance.html
www.fsc.org/fileadmin/web-data/public/document_center/publications/fact_sheets/
Notes_on_the_early years_of_FSC_by_Tim_Synnott.pdf

# 10 BOARDS

In private companies the primary function of the Board is to represent the shareholders (strictly it is to serve the interests of the company – but law has steadily evolved towards seeing board directors as shareholder representatives). The Board members are appointed by the shareholders, and they in turn appoint the chief executive, and monitor the company on behalf of the shareholders. In the social economy it is the mission that is central rather than shareholders (if there are any). The function of the board in a charity is to be a guardian of that charitable mission (as well as ensuring that the organisation is solvent, and abiding by the law). Yet in the stories of social entrepreneurs, Boards rarely feature. From this perspective it is the entrepreneurial driver who is the primary interpreter of the mission in practice. It is to the mission that he or she is accountable. If the test of accountability is what can be practically achieved (and financed), on what basis can a non-executive Board of a social venture challenge the chief executive? To whom or to what is the Board accountable?

The David Hubbard Memorial Library at the Fuller Theological
Seminary in Pasadena, California, designed by the ecological architect,
William McDonough.

David Hubbard was a past President of the seminary, the largest
interdenominational seminary in the world. A theological scholar, who
was described as a man of 'unlimited peripheral vision', he developed
a distinct view and practice for his Board. He saw them as one of three
centres of power in the institution, alongside the President and his
office, and the faculty, all of them bound by the seminary's mission.
The Board members were governors, financial contributors, ambassadors
and consultants.

Hubbard saw the President's job as divided between overseeing his vice
presidents, and relating to the trustees. He had a full time assistant to
care for the trustees and encouraged his staff to brief and orient them.
He established sub-committees chaired by a Trustee with whom he
worked closely. He took them on study tours. He ensured that any
problems in the seminary and its affiliates were given more prominence
in Board meetings than the good news. He reserved one hour at every
Board for the trustees to set the agenda. And all this within a trustee
time commitment of some ten days a year.

For him the process of joint leadership with a Board was as central to
the outcome – whether in a seminary or in hospital care – as any other
single task.

The private sector has struggled with the issue of governance. Some entrepreneurial firms have largely cosmetic boards, while some big firms have boards effectively controlled by their Chief Executives. Then there are periods when the boards hit back – like the waves of sackings that took place in the early 2000s ('Revolt in the Boardroom').

If this is the case with private sector boards, then the issue is even more complex in a social venture. But whether private or social, there is one general point to keep in mind. It is that all organisational governance is a compromise between competing principles – flexibility and speed versus scrutiny; entrepreneurialism versus hierarchy; specialised divisions of labour versus generalist oversight; accountability versus freedom.

## Accountability

One view of social accountability, that mirrors the role of private company Boards, is that the Board of a social venture represents those who have given money to it. A second one is the stakeholder Board (see **method 9**) that is accountable to those who are required to make the venture a success. A third alternative is that a Board is accountable to those to whom its mission is directed – members of a co-op for example, children (or their parents) in a school, or patients in a hospital. Co-ops have a long tradition of how to make this real, with the Board accountable to meetings of members, or, in larger co-ops, to representatives of members. Representation, with all its advantages and limitations, is the key issue here, akin to the parallel problem in political democratic forms.

The problem of representation arises for all social ventures whose beneficiaries are a community who do not know each other. In the case of environmental ventures, the beneficiaries are generalised – the planet and its peoples – including the generations yet to be born. Any notion of accountability has to be framed in terms of those who are socially recognised as legitimate interpreters of such a mission.

In other cases the constituency is more specific. NHS Hospital Trusts, for example, have made an effort to include patients on the Board but with only limited success, since the patients are not a self defining community. Room 13 on the other hand, a social enterprise originating in Fort William, Scotland that over 15 years has generated an international network of independent art studios within schools, has children as the de facto boards for each studio. It is the children who appoint the resident artists and are responsible for raising and managing the funds for the project. As with Janusz Korczac's celebrated story of King Matt the First, a kingdom runs very differently when a child is in charge.[3]

The first point to make then is that the boards of social ventures have a much less clearly defined role and mission than the board of a private market company. There is a less tightly defined mission, and an ambiguity about accountability, about who is to interpret that mission. This creates a space for the fruitful interplay of different views. It is also the space for conflict. Our view is that it is important to have the venture's constituency strongly represented in the governance structures – charity law needs to be updated to permit this to happen as a norm rather than an exception – but that is only one part of the story.

## The separation of authority and activity

Whatever its composition, there is a deeper structural problem for Boards, not least for private companies. The great American management thinker Peter Drucker took this view and said that the decline of the Board – irrespective of its legal form – was a universal phenomenon of the 20th century. The executives dominate the Board, often determining who is the chairman and the non-executives (exemplified in the Enron case). They control the company and its information. They are the performers on the field of play. The company's welfare depends on them, and the non-executive Board members as bystanders are always at a disadvantage. The tension between owners and managers, long recognised in managerial economics, is played out as a tension between non executive board members and staff.[2]

If this is the case for private company boards, with their formal clarity of role and purpose, there is an even greater problem with social venture boards. John Carver, a US writer who has spent his life studying and advising on public and not for profit organisations – in schools, hospitals, arts organisations, clubs, foundations, councils and commissions – concluded that almost without exception they were performing "at a distressingly low percentage of their leadership potential".[3]

He describes voluntary board members arriving at the table with dreams, but then having to live through a nightmare. He found that boards spent time on the trivial, that they have a short term and reactive bias, that they review, rehash and attempt to redo, and that they tend to be·completely overloaded with inoperable detail. Authority is diffuse and accountability leaky. He concluded that boards were usually either cheer-leaders that rubber stamped executive decisions or over-involved in the detail of management.

His answer is that boards should focus on fundamental values, on the vision and the mission and on driving through the outcomes. They should force an external orientation and encourage forward thinking. They should relate to the key constituencies, and spend more time in creating (leading) than approving.[4]

These functions are echoed by many of the commentators on not for profit governance. They refer to what are desirable features in any organisation. But they do not address the central fault line between the full time staff and an occasional board.

There are still traces in these commentaries of the 20th century division between those who plan and those who do, between mental and manual labour, or in social economy terms between moral and manual labour. This is what makes the approaches of these commentaries so different from the writings of social entrepreneurs. For the latter the question is not one of vision, or ethics, or mission, but how to generate projects which embody these goals. Andrew Mawson of the Bromley-by-Bow Centre says that he sees all his activity as having the character of an art work (see the Introduction above). From that perspective, putting a Board in charge of the vision and its realisation of a social venture would be like putting an art critic in charge of a studio.

## Beyond the divide

The answer we recommend is to start not with a hierarchical division of authority, but from the project and how it ensures the fruitful interplay of reflection and practice, how it creates not only shared values but a shared culture about how it develops as a venture. We call this a shared organisational pragmatism.

Those on the Board can play an important part in this process. They will have a range of experiences, and be part of different networks. They may have limited time, but in the time they have they should be seen first and foremost not as governors, but as active innovators. They should be artists rather than critics.

In the period of establishing a new venture Board members will in effect be volunteer staff, working alongside both paid and unpaid staff and consultants. They will have an active role in day to day operations, helping in the establishment of financial systems and budgets, the drafting of contracts and leases, the raising of finance, the development of the venture's information systems and metrics and so on. Later their time may best be spent less in day to day operations than in long run planning and playing a role in keeping the venture open (**method 18**). But like David Hubbard's Board, it is still helpful for them to be involved with one part of the venture's operations – to be a creative force rather than a governing bystander.

The critical condition for this to work is for the Board to be part of the processes of formation (**method 20**). This involves both activity and reflection. Just as members of the Board should be involved in activities, so they should engage in the reflexive work of the organisation, in the understanding and continual re-interpretation of its work. There is even a case for having a second quasi Board, with overlapping membership, responsible for the development of the venture's process of reflection and formation, and the clarification and deepening of its mission. The primary Board would be responsible for operations, the shadow Board for its process of learning.

It is striking how many successful social ventures establish some form of academy that performs this reflective function. In the Lynedoch eco-village it was at the very heart of the village (**method 2**). Sekem has established a university (**method 18**) as has Mondragon (**method 13**). Younger, smaller ventures need some micro structure to ensure that this function is not crowded out by the demands of day to day operations. It is not enough to assign this task even partially to the Board. The task and its integration with operations has to involve both the Board and the staff.[7]

Only through such engagement with a social venture's activity and reflection can Board members hope to avoid the tension between staff and board. In this sense they have a double identity. On the one hand they are volunteers working within the project team, and part of the organisational super-ego – the processes that develop the critical and moral function that is necessary for an organisation's integrated identity. On the other, they play a practical governance role within the project team – approving accounts, agreeing budgets, and making key appointments. They also act as a dispute resolver of last resort, but if the formation process is working this should be a rare task.

Instead of viewing a Board in terms of hierarchical power, we see it rather as part of a continuum of engagement. At one end of the spectrum are those with only occasional engagement with the venture, at the other those engaged full time, centring on the key drivers of the innovation. The Board are a category of volunteers who devote a tithe of their time, say 20-30 days a year, to ensuring the success of the venture. It is not an occasional exercise of power, but a contribution to the creation of that power.

Boards as instruments of governance of social ventures have a dysfunctional history. They represent a division between moral and manual labour and authority, when the success of a social venture depends on an integration of the two. The means of overcoming this division is in part through participation in an active process of formation, and in part through the engagement of Board members in the operational work of the venture.

References
- Peter Drucker, Managing the Non Profit Organisation, Collins 2005
- J.Gregory Dees, Jed Emerson and Peter Economy, Strategic Tools for Social Entrepreneurs, John Wiley, 2002, Chapter 5
- J.Carver, Boards that Make a Difference, Jossey-Bass, 3rd edition 2006

Links
www.room13scotland.com/room13network.php

End notes

1   Korczak was a doctor who set up a remarkable orphanage in Warsaw in the 1930s. He and the orphans died in the gas chambers of Treblinka, but the story of the orphanage and the pedagogic principles developed by Korczac have lived on and remain a significant influence on education and more generally on how adults relate to children. See Janusz Korczak, King Matt the First, Vintage 2005, and Betty Jean Lifton, The King of Children: The Life and Death of Janusz Korczak, American Academy of Pediatrics, 2005. In the Korczak's story of King Matt, a child succeeds his father and insists on ruling himself on behalf of children rather than through counsellors. In the end the adults overthrow him.

2   The Cadbury Committee in the early 1990s was one of a number of responses to the unease over corporate governance and made a range of proposals about how the composition and conduct of corporate boards could be improved. This helped but the limitations of Boards has again been thrown into relief not just by Enron but also by the absence of effective control of banks by their Boards over the past decade. Cadbury, Sir A., Committee on Financial Aspects of Corporate Governance, HMSO 1992.

3   John Carver, Boards that Make a Difference, Jossey-Bass, 3rd edition, 2006. Preface p.xxi

4   Ibid pp 30-31 for a summary. These points relate to a Board's function. Other recommendations concern the way the Board operates.

5   Philip Pullman's novel Northern Lights takes features of the human psyche and embodies them in a different person, as though the anima was separate from the other parts of the self. Every character in the novel has his or her own daemon, a separate soul. All social ventures need their own distinct anima.

# SECTION 3: RAISING THE FINANCE

Financing a new venture requires money to cover three things:

- the cost of tangible capital investment like buildings and equipment

- the start-up deficits until the venture breaks even

- the working capital necessary to cover the gap between trading payments and receipts.

For social ventures it is the second of these that is the main challenge. It requires backers who share the venture's mission and are patient about its outcome. Where the new venture is innovative there is likely to be a particular challenge, since it usually takes time for the model to mature into its most effective form (the same challenge is faced in business).

Social ventures also face a challenge of how to fund the build up of intangibles. Relationships, trust, networks, reliability all take time. Developing a supply chain, a brand, a core staff or a network of support are all social, and call for the skills of the community organiser rather than the engineer (see Section 4 below). The harvest of these intangible investments may be reflected in financial results, but equally may represent the non-financial benefits of the venture.

Some ventures separate the functions of developing the social intangibles into a separate company funded by grant aid and the profits of the income earning venture. This was the case with the Lynedoch eco-village (see **method 2**). In fair trade, many of the companies have a charitable arm that works with producers to strengthen their capacity to trade and diversify, and to expand the knowledge of fair trade in the North. Sometimes it is the social venture funded from grants that spins off a commercial project that requires its own funding. For all of them there is an interweaving of grants, commercial loans, and some form of equity.

The key to social venture financing is two-fold:

- to align the goals of the finance with the mission of the venture

- to find forms of finance that strengthen the enterprise through the skills and networks that come with it and add fire to the flame of the idea and the narrative on which the venture is based.

# 11 FINANCING NEW VENTURES

The first over-riding rule in the financing of social ventures is that the sources of core finance should share the venture's social goals as the primary driver of the enterprise. The question is how to achieve this.

The chair of the fair trade company Divine Chocolate Ltd presents a dividend cheque to the President of the Kuapa Kokoo Union for £47,379, as Kuapa Kokoo's 45 per cent share of the Divine dividend for the year 2007.

Kuapa Kokoo, who supply the cocoa for Divine Chocolate, is a union of 45,000 cocoa farmers, organised in 1,200 village societies. The challenge of how to ensure the union's stake in the equity when it had so little capital to invest was solved by issuing only a limited number of common shares (originally 99 £1 shares, now 122 £1 shares) and raising the initial capital almost entirely through loan stock and preference shares.

Those contributing to the initial round of funding had a certain portion of the equity and in some cases a seat on the Board, but the device of the limited common shares meant that the producers could not only afford to pay for their shares, but they had a primary say in the governance of the company and have been able to retain a major stake in the appreciation of its capital.

Initially the company was heavily indebted because of its reliance on loan funding and subordinated debt. But after 10 years successful trading, it is in the ordinary shares that most value resides. In 2006, the last time shares in Divine Chocolate were traded, shares were bought for £33,333 each, which would value Kuapa Kokoo's stake at around £1.8 million.

In the grant economy, there should not be a problem. We would expect grants to be given only if the donor supported the venture's goals. But in the social market, equity finance may come from many sources, and it is the alignment of this finance with the social goals that is the main challenge.

## Safeguarding equity

One answer is to have the equity contributed by the initiators and/or beneficiaries of the enterprise, and seek external funds only in the form of loans and preference shares. This was the path followed by Divine Chocolate.

A similar outcome can be achieved by capitalising contributions in kind. So-called sweat equity recognises the value of voluntary labour in an enterprise, or other non-financial contributions made in setting up an enterprise.

There is another version that we call 'soft equity'. In fair trade, producers have offered to contribute small sums over time. This can take the form of a small deduction from the sale of their commodities or the investment of the fair trade premium received on the sale of goods (as was the case with the coffee and tea producers in Cafédirect).

Or charities may fund the equity stake of beneficiaries (The Hunter Foundation and Comic Relief have both followed this route). In other cases the initiators of the enterprise have gifted shares to the beneficiaries, to ensure they have a direct stake in the success of the enterprise (this is how the banana producers first got their 50 per cent stake in the fair trade fruit company, Agrofair).

Co-ops have financed their equity in many of these ways – through the pooling of their own funds, through sweat equity, and other contributions in kind.

All these are ways of establishing and funding equity that retains a major stake for the beneficiaries and/or the social entrepreneurs. It ensures their voice in the key decisions of the enterprise, as well as a share in its financial success. But for the beneficiaries it does something more. Their equity stake is the basis for a more reciprocal relationship between the partners than is the case with a charity. The goals of the enterprise may be similar to those of the charity, but the economic and governance relations are quite different.

That said, it remains the case that those with little capital usually need more than they can contribute themselves. Where can they get it on terms which support rather than supplant the social mission as the primary imperative?

## Ethical finance

One potential source is ethical banks. These have grown rapidly over the last 20 years, and have been important sources of capital for social enterprises. They have contributed valuable technical and financial advice in addition to finance – assisting in the formulation of business plans and the financial sustainability of the enterprises in which they invest. But they have one occupational hazard. They remain banks in the sense that the primary assessment of their operations is financial. They may offer capital where mainstream banks will not, and on better terms than the norm. They may be more 'patient' and long term in their expectation of returns. But in the end it is the financial returns that are determining.

One of the first questions put by potential ethical investors are the terms of exit. How can they withdraw their capital, expanded by the success of the enterprise, to repay those from whom they draw their own funds, or to invest in the next enterprise? This is the perspective of money capital. It makes it hesitant to finance start-ups, and where it does so it seeks higher returns (and a larger slice of equity) to offset the greater risks.

It is a perspective that is a necessary dimension of a social enterprise operating in the market economy. It needs financial discipline and to generate a surplus for further investment. If it borrows from commercial banks it expects to pay a market rate of interest. What is at issue, however, is whether the imperative of financial expansion comes to dominate over the primacy of the social goals. The danger for a social enterprise is that a reliance for core funding on capital whose primary purpose is financial self expansion – whether from banks or venture funds – will commonly lead to the financial imperative dominating its conduct and strategy.

This is as much an issue of differing perspectives within a private market economy, as it is of private versus social enterprises operating in the market. In Anglo Saxon capitalism, the financial perspective has traditionally dominated. But in the industrial districts of Germany and Italy, as well as in the manufacturing sectors of Japan, it is the productive view that is to the fore. Firms will focus on innovation and where that positions them in relation to international competition, and only then call in the finance director. The view of the economy in terms of production tends to be longer term in its outlook than the financial view.

Social enterprises in this sense are like the family firms in Europe's industrial districts or the Japanese zaibatsu. Social enterprises have a predominantly use value perspective on the economy – not just in respect of production, but in terms of the nature of the product and its social and/or environmental impact. This is the driver, not the maximisation of returns, and needs to be reflected in the equity structure and the terms of finance.

There are a wide range of ethical banks and social funding agencies. Many have devoted themselves to supporting new and expanding ventures in ways that place the enterprise's material development to the fore and reduce risk as a result. Our remarks are thus framed as questions to all sources of finance and their role as core funders, rather than a critique of ethical banks as such.

In order to ensure that initial venture funding remains instrumental and subordinate to the values and distributional principles of social projects, enterprises can raise social equity, limit the quantity of common shares, and seek subordinated loans from sources ready to share early risk without demanding a counterbalancing share in the project's equity.

References

Bob Doherty and Sophi Tranchell "New thinking in international trade: a case study of the Day Chocolate Company", Sustainable Development, Vol 13, 3, June 2005 pp 166-176

# 12 PUBLIC SHARE ISSUES

In mainstream financial markets share issues are a means of raising finance. For social enterprise they are also a way of encouraging social and political engagement.

Your own noise sounds different to other people's. This has been the lesson of the growth of wind power in Western Europe. It has proceeded fastest where the windmills have been owned and established by community co-operatives, as was the case in Denmark where 75 per cent of all wind turbines were co-operatively owned, and in Germany. In Denmark when a new government came in 2001 and changed the regulations to disadvantage small scale ownership of windpower, protests against new wind turbines rose, and expansion slowed. Here is one of Britain's few co-operatively owned wind farms at Westmill in Oxfordshire. It has 2,400 shareholders, many of whom turned out to celebrate the launch of the wind farm – seen above – a few miles from the coal fired Didcot power station.

The last 25 years has seen social enterprises making an innovative use of public share issues. Between 1984 and 2003 there were 37, half of them by ethical banks and funds.

Carefully designed they have been found to have many benefits, and one defect. The benefits are:

- capital provided on terms aligned with the social mission of the enterprise

- a network of investors who can offer many different types of support other than finance

- a forum of accountability to those who have invested in the social mission of the enterprise

The defect is cost. The regulations developed over a century to prevent fraudulent or misleading appeals to the public for equity finance, are now so cumbersome as to require a massive input of time and professional fees in issuing a prospectus and conducting a launch, in addition to the marketing costs of the launch itself. From our experience the minimum cost is £150,000 for a start-up company, and up to £600,000 for a small company expanding its capital base.

## The attraction of social returns

Yet the advantages are considerable. First, the capital. In four of the leading cases from the sample of 37, all raised between £4 million and £6 million and all were oversubscribed. The Ethical Property Company which invests in commercial premises to provide cheap office space to social enterprises and organisations, has had three share issues which have together raised £15 million. The Westmill Wind Co-operative raised £4.4 million to build five wind turbines in Oxfordshire, and received so many applications that it had to ration the shares (giving priority to those living within 50 miles of the windmills). The two fair trade companies, Traidcraft and Cafédirect, raised £4 million and £4.5 million respectively.

In each case the returns offered were modest. Westmill Wind forecast that there would be no returns for five years, and then a rising scale from five per cent upto 25 per cent by the 25th year, paid from the sale of electricity generated by the wind turbines. This projected flow of income – itself subject to technical and economic risks – if discounted over 25 years would yield a rate of return that was lower than a commercial investor would expect. Both Traidcraft and

Cafédirect were explicit in the prospectus that dividends would be modest –
three per cent to four per cent in the case of Cafédirect – since the priority was
re-investment for the benefit of the producers.

That was one disincentive for conventional capital. A second that was notable
in the two fair trade companies was that their principal assets were intangible
and not reflected in the balance sheet. In the case of Traidcraft, the company
grew through its links to a large number of church groups who would sell their
products at church gatherings and other local events. In the case of Cafédirect,
it had developed not only the most widely known fair trade brand, but through
one of its founders, Twin Trading, was supplied by co-operatives many of
whom had relationships with the company extending back a decade. It was
these relationships that made Cafédirect so distinct from other coffee
companies. None of these intangibles were reflected on the balance sheet,
but they were the things that were the potential attraction for investors.

City analysts – even those connected to ethical funds – found it difficult to take
the Cafédirect share offer seriously. They regarded the company as overvalued
(in spite of high profitability) with little prospects of commercial dividends. Yet
the share issue attracted 4,300 subscribers, each investing an average of just
over £1,000 each, similar to the experience of Traidcraft. With Westmill, which
at least promised a tangible asset in the form of five wind turbines, there were
nearly 2,400 investors, averaging just under £2,000 each.

Here then was a substantial group of small investors, whose primary interest
was in the goals of the company. Cafédirect had decided on a share issue
after the collapse of negotiations with its first option for raising new capital –
a Dutch ethical venture fund. The fund had raised its finance on the promise
of a 15 per cent rate of return to its investors over 10 years. Adding to this
the costs of running the fund, and of covering the costs of firms in the fund's
portfolio that failed, meant that they were looking for 25 per cent annual
returns. These were low by conventional venture capital standards, but
crippling for Cafédirect. During the negotiations it was clear that Cafédirect
would have to focus on its financial returns were the venture fund to become
a significant shareholder. It would re-orient the company, however sympathetic
the fund's intentions. The share issue on the other hand re-enforced the social
mission as the company's primary concern.

## Shareholders as a support network

The attraction of a large group of sympathetic shareholders is important not
just as a source of capital. They also constitute a significant resource. In the
case of Westmill, the organic farmer who pioneered the scheme, had faced

national opposition from interests opposed to wind power. The farmer explained the environmental case for wind to those in the neighbourhood, and pointed out that this was to be a co-operatively owned project so that they could share in the benefits. The opposition dissolved, planning permission was granted, and local shareholders now provide a base of continuing support.

In such cases a share issue is a way of offering those anyway engaged in or affected by a project to have a direct stake in it, and to attract new supporters. Many of those who acted as informal sellers of Traidcraft's products became investors. Tenants of the Ethical Property Company invested in the share issue. Cafédirect's shareholders offered to give talks, chivvy supermarkets, and volunteer when needed. In other words, a public share issue is a way of radically extending a network of support.

Lastly, such groups of shareholders represent in an informal way the interests of the social mission of the enterprise. The company executives, faced with contending pressures, have to keep to the fore the aspirations of such shareholders. Annual General meetings – unusually well attended – are primarily geared to reports on the social impact of the enterprise rather than its finances. They represent one element of a system of social accountability.

Not all social enterprises need to be attached to wider networks. But there are many where the fact that they embody social aspirations means they can draw on commitment and support in a way that private firms cannot. Shareholding provides one of a number of frameworks for organising that support a sense of common ownership in the project.

## Widening shareholding

From this perspective, it is important that the size of the minimum shareholding is not set too high so that it does not exclude those with little capital. The Grameen principle is relevant here. Subscriptions should be welcomed, however small, and they can be added to. In local regeneration projects, for example, the fact that anyone in the neighbourhood can purchase a share in a development trust, and gain from the appreciation of assets that results from the scheme is one way in which a community can feel subjects rather than objects of a programme.

Those running an enterprise hesitate to go down this route. Organising a large number of small shareholders is a job in itself and their priority is the business. But we should listen to many of the most successful social enterprises who recognise that such networks of support are part of the business. The Big Issue depends on such networks. Divine Chocolate has more than 50,000 children organised as Dubble agents involved in its Dubble brand. Extensive shareholding is a similar means of engagement.

## Organising shareholders

In the age of the internet, organising large numbers of people and having them represented as shareholders becomes easier. One way of doing so is through co-operative structures. Co-ops – like the Japanese food co-ops – have their own structures of representation which could well be emulated by other social enterprises. At the time of the Cafédirect share issue, there was a plan to organise an investor/consumer co-op with its own representation on the Board, but the executive was hesitant because of the costs and complexity (this was 2003) and it has yet to be implemented. As the number of social enterprises expands we expect increasing use to be made of public share issues, and for these enterprises to find innovative ways of engaging small shareholders in their operations and the determination of their strategic direction.

## Loyalty, voice and exit

With mainstream shareholding, a small shareholder has little voice but ease of exit. For the most part entry and exit is determined financially. With social enterprises, public shareholding has limited scope for exit, but in principle greater voice.

There have been attempts to establish a social stock market which to date have not been realised. Instead there is a system of matched bargains at a posted price. A price is set and those wishing to sell at that price must wait until there are buyers. As yet the turnover of shares has been small. For in general those who have invested have done so on the basis of their commitment to the vision of the enterprise, and if and when the firm diverts from this vision, they are more likely to voice their concerns than to sell their shares. Shareholders in social enterprises do not split finance from production. As a result the shares are less liquid, but the shareholders are more engaged and with longer horizons of time.

Public share issues are most suitable at times of expansion, when the enterprise has proved itself, and risks are reduced. They have the advantage over venture capital funding in that they can tap investors who are ready to make social impact the primary incentive rather than financial returns. To paraphrase Oliver Cromwell, they offer a means to trust in God while keeping their financial powder dry. There has been a notable growth of micro lending over the past forty years. Public share issues are one form of a new movement for micro borrowing.

# 13 LOAN FINANCE

Initial capital is usually a mix of equity and loans. For the enterprise, equity has the advantage of not demanding interest charges during the build up period. For social enterprises it presents the challenge of alignment. For them the ideal finance is some form of subordinated debt, preference shares or loans that do not require dividends or interest until the enterprise is profitable. It is often possible to get subscribers of equity to provide some parallel subordinated debt. But many social enterprises will need to rely on interest bearing loans for some of their capital needs. This poses questions not just of the loan terms, but of risk, and forms of security.

The town of Mondragon in the Basque region of Spain has over the past 50 years developed a network of 140 workers co-ops employing over 100,000 people and making everything from washing machines to bicycles, and microchips to bullet trains. Central to their growth has been the Caja Laboral, the network's bank that provides credit to the co-ops it has helped to nurture. This could be called venture lending rather than venture capital, since the bank in its formative period provided extensive forms of technical support to the developing co-ops, but without asking for an equity stake. The principle of the group is that capital should be 'instrumental and subordinated' to the core values of the groups which are the education and sovereignty of the producers. The Mondragon group is now the third largest industrial group in Spain.

Lenders, without an equity stake, will normally require some form of collateral to minimise their risk. The most common form of security is a charge over some or all the company's assets. The asset may be property, and finance is advanced in the manner of a corporate mortgage, with lending upto a set proportion of the value of the property (say 70 per cent) and rights to take over the property and sell it to realise the outstanding loan. Or it may be current assets, such as stocks or debtors, with loans advanced, as with property, up to a stated portion of the total. Invoice discounting has been resorted to by many social enterprises – an expensive but available source of funds.

All this is mainstream finance, open to social enterprise, with the customary caveats about a robust business plan and sufficient equity to act as a buffer in the event of the financial misfortune of the enterprise. Banks do not want to get into the details of management – unlike venture capital – and therefore prefer a wide margin of security to limit their risk. As social enterprises are often considered more risky, it is the ethical banks like Shared Interest, Cordaid, Oikocredit or Root Capital that have provided these kinds of facilities. From their point of view it is a relatively low risk way of supporting the social enterprises they are established to promote.

There are three other ways of reducing the lender's risk that have specific relevance to social enterprises:

* guarantees

* saving/lender unions

* contracts

## Guarantees

Financial risk is in the eye of the beholder. It reflects – in part at least – the extent to which a lender knows the borrower. The knowledge may be statistical, through credit records and rating agencies. But it is those who know those launching the social enterprise personally who are in the best position to estimate the qualities and risks of the people involved and to balance this against their assessment of the merits of the project. In these cases they do not need to subscribe to the capital, but rather, provide guarantees against which a loan can be raised.

Guarantees of this kind have been extensively used in Italy through the formation of guarantee co-operatives, known as 'consorzio fidi', designed to address the problem of financing of co-operatives and other small and medium firms. The Modena consortia is typical. Its members elect a committee – commonly the most respected entrepreneurs from each sector. A proposal is studied by the relevant committee member from the sector in question (clothing, furniture, engineering, food processing and so on) and they give their judgement on the quality of the proposal and the capacity of the proposer. Where the recommendation is positive the committee then undertakes to guarantee a bank loan to the enterprise, backed by a small capital reserve and the personal guarantees of each member of the consortia.

It has been a remarkably successful type of institution, with failure rates of less than 0.5 per cent as against seven per cent for the mainstream financial sector. Part of the reason is the first hand knowledge of the borrowers and the specialist assessment of the project (too few banks have this degree of sector specialism) and part is the borrower's sense of obligation to repay. In the words of one of the Modena borrowers "when I borrow from a bank I lie awake at night wondering how not to pay back the loan, but when I borrow through the consortia I lie awake at night thinking how to pay." The nexus is one of both knowledge and obligation.

There is scope for the extension of these principles to the funding of social enterprises. The Centre for Alternative Technology at Machynlleth used financial guarantees from its supporters to back one of its loan applications. Divine Chocolate raised an initial £500,000 loan finance from NatWest with an 80 per cent guarantee from the then Ministry of Overseas Development (it required a special Act of Parliament to allow this). Public bodies have by and large been reluctant to provide guarantees because the sums are set against their capital budget, but Sheffield City Council found an innovative way around this public finance accounting practice by promising to pay its guarantee on any default in the following financial year. We could imagine a group of shareholders or supporters coming together, electing a committee as in Modena, and providing a collective guarantee for approved projects.

## Saving/Lender Unions

Similar principles underlie credit unions and social banks where the borrowers are savers and known to each other. The largest in Canada is that of the Menonites, which operates an internal economy quite separate from mainstream finance. Savers receive considerably less than the normal rate of interest, but in turn can borrow at low rates and this helped their rapid extension of land ownership and enterprise formation in the 1990s. As in Modena, these loans took place within a community with strong social bonds and a consequent sense of obligation.

A parallel example is the Caja Laboral in Mondragon mentioned above. A condition for any eventual loan was that the enterprise deposited its finance and the savings of its members in the Caja Laboral itself, ensuring the circular flow of money between the firms, their members and the bank.

## Market outlets

One of the main sources of risk for any new enterprise is its performance in the market. It can control its costs, but its markets are little more than speculative. Anything that can reduce this risk increases the possibility of loans.

The best of all options is a long term contract, something that a purchaser will be hesitant to give to a start-up. But many of the innovations in this field have come from local government, developing new services with social enterprises financed by loans backed by the contract. There have been pitfalls to this way of working. Contracting rules tends to overspecify practices in services which are in the process of development. The client officers may change and collapse the collaborative relationship. But this kind of collaborative development is likely to expand in the next decade, and open up a new source of core financing for social enterprise as a result.

In the market economy such initial contracts are harder to come by, but here the opportunity is for collaboration between a social enterprise and a retailer. One version of this has been pioneered by the Quaker firm Clarks Shoes, the largest shoe retailer in the UK. They have offered guaranteed outlets for The Soul of Africa, a social enterprise set up in South Africa, to manufacture shoes with the profits distributed to those suffering from AIDS. With this support, the enterprise has achieved a turnover of £0.5 million in two years, and its financibility as a result.

A similar scheme has been pioneered by DFID, the UK's ministry for international development. Their FRICH programme provides financial support to collaborations between retailers and importers that offer markets for African primary producers. It reflects the growing recognition that it is secure markets that provide the basis for the upgrading and expansion of African primary producers, as well as their finance. As fair trade has demonstrated, start of season contracts have enabled producer co-operatives to raise pre- and post-harvest finance both from overseas and domestic banks.

The social economy has developed distinct forms of lending which draw on the goals and social networks that characterise so many of its projects. One is to create a saving and lending circle separated from the commercial financial market, in which savers become borrowers, and borrowers savers. Another is for supporters of projects to provide guarantees to commercial lenders – a kind of social economy insurance rather than the provision of cash. A third is to drive lending through sales contracts or guaranteed income streams that in some cases could be securitised as a means for raising capital. Many of these involve a strong sense of social connection and obligation as a means of lowering the cost of finance.

References
www.sfsgo.com/guaranteecompany.asp

# **14** SOCIAL IMPACT BONDS

Finding a way to connect the finance of a project or enterprise with a financial value of its social impact has generated a long line of initiatives by governments. The UK Government's Invest to Save programme was one recent one, Public Service Agreements are another. There are trading schemes which aim to provide a means for quantifying environmental impact in cash terms – carbon credits and Packaging Recovery Notes for example. Social Impact Bonds are a further variant of these public finance innovations.

The Aylesbury estate in Southwark, South London, with 10,000 residents, was the largest housing estate in Western Europe. It was built as a model of urban design in the 1960s, with raised pedestrian walkways, combined heat and power, a health centre and dedicated waste cupboards outside every house. Forty years later its fabric was crumbling, the waste cupboards were trashed, there were high rates of ill health, crime, unemployment and drug dealing.

It transpired there was no way of accounting for the public money that could be saved by cross cutting projects that addressed the root causes of the problems. There was no way of aggregating the cost to the public purse of housing, social welfare, unemployment, police, fire, the health service, even the private bus services laid on by the local council to transport their workers safely to and from the estate. And therefore no way of linking project finance to public savings. In 2005 it was decided to demolish the estate.

Social Impact Bonds are a financial tool being developed in the UK (by the Young Foundation and Social Finance) to provide a new way to invest money in social outcomes. Their key innovation is to link investments (by commercial investors or foundations); a programme of actions to improve the prospects of a particular group (for example 14-16 year olds in a particular area at risk of crime or unemployment); and commitments by national government to make payments linked to outcomes achieved in improving the lives of the group (for example, lower numbers in prison, and lower benefits payments). The concept is being developed in collaboration with national and local government as well as foundations and will be piloted shortly. Related work is underway in the Young Foundation social value programme.

## Finance for social outcomes

Many forms of finance go towards achieving social outcomes – mainstream public spending of all kinds, grants, loans, equity investments by RDAs and convertible grants. There is growing interest in more innovative approaches to finance ranging from advance market commitments (AMCs) for purchasing of pharmaceuticals to local bonds (for example in Sheffield), to the burgeoning field of social investment.

## Misaligned incentives

In the UK there has long been particular interest in designing new financial tools to address misaligned incentives in social policy, for example:

- that local authorities or NGOs responsible for providing services to young people do not share the benefits from reductions in prison numbers or benefits bills

- that there are few incentives for agencies to invest heavily in early years support, despite strong evidence on the long-term social gains

- that health prevention often involves action by agencies such as schools which have inadequate incentives to act

## Past experiments

These misalignments prompted many of the experiments with joined-up government in the 1990s and 2000s (such as the UK government's Rough Sleepers Unit which pooled budgets), and there have been many innovative approaches designed to both map and realign the costs and benefits associated with actions. A recent example of an attempt to do this was a revised 'Green Book' for investment developed by the UK government in the early 2000s to compare investments in programmes like SureStart, training for teenagers and higher education in terms of a Net Present Value (NPV). The aim of this exercise was to capture the full range of potential costs and benefits, and to provide an equivalent guide to those which already exist for capital investment in such things as roads and railways. In practice however the range of uncertainties was too wide to make this useable. Other simpler approaches to the same problem have involved contracting, including the many examples of outcomes-based budgeting in Scandinavia and around the world. A notable UK example has been the Employment Zones which directly incentivised contractors to achieve outcomes in helping long-term unemployed people back to work, and more recently outcome based budgeting has been used in contracts around offending.

## The Three Models

Drawing on these lessons work has been underway to investigate the potential for new financial devices to better align incentives. This has pointed to three categories of approach which we loosely label Social Impact Bonds, in that they involve some borrowing with repayment linked to success in achieving social impacts.

## Local authority Social Impact Bonds

A local authority borrows for a package of investment in a social impact programme (e.g. for teenagers at risk of NEET status) and receives a series of payments from national government if particular milestones are achieved associated with lower costs for national government. For example, a city or London borough would borrow £5m for an intensive programme of work with NEETs or potential young offenders, and would be repaid according to the numbers who achieved educational qualifications relative to an agreed baseline of similar local authorities. The repayments would represent a proportion of the lifetime savings to national government (primarily through tax and benefits). Models of this kind are relatively easy to design and implement, involve relatively few players and transaction costs, though they would require clear protocols on design, establishment of baselines, success measures and so on.

## Commissioning for social outcomes

Another model is to directly incentivise a service provider or group of providers to take responsibility for part of an age cohort in a particular area, e.g. 5 per cent of 14 year olds, with direct incentives to achieve educational and other goals by 19. This would extend the Employment Zone model, and again is relatively easy to design. Contractors would raise their own capital either through social investment sources (in which case they might be described as Social Impact Bonds) or on the market. In the latter case there might be some risk sharing with an investor (such as a foundation). In all of these cases there are some important issues around risk transfer (and important lessons to be learned from the problems associated with PFIs, private prisons etc) as well as issues of accountability (in particular the local authority's responsibility for children).

## Full Social Impact Bonds

A third alternative would share the risk for a bundle of interventions, with:

- finance raised from the market, with investors taking some of the risk for non-achievement of social outcomes

- action through a special purpose vehicle (potentially combining public sector, private and third sector) to manage a series of interventions with a target group

- and, again, payments based on results against benchmarks.

This model is somewhat more complex, with more handovers and transaction costs, but opens up a radical new avenue for bringing in new sources of finance.

Several fields have been proposed for bonds of this kind. These range from investment in early years programmes (based on the evidence from the Abecedarian and High/Scope Perry Pre-school Programmes for substantial long-term paybacks), to NEETs (focused on life time earnings) and youth or young adult offending; care leavers; and investments in health prevention and improvement. Another potential field for action is in employment creation during the downturn.

In principle the model is likely to work best in the short to medium term where:

- there is a reasonably short gap between interventions and measurable results

- there are very tangible financial gains – for example the very high costs associated with prison places, as well as with crime

- the numbers of players are small, i.e. one primary national department, a local authority, finance body and other agencies working on contract.

## Challenges

There are three main challenges for any financing device of this kind:

*   measurement – agreed baselines and metrics that are not vulnerable
    to economic downturns, national policy changes (e.g. new crimes being
    legislated), and shared analysis of lifetime costs and benefits associated
    with different actions and client groups

*   action – all depend on there being a credible menu of actions to implement
    which significantly outperform existing ones, and they also depend on
    the presence of an implementation capacity. In most cases this is likely
    to involve a mix of public, private and voluntary organisations – in none
    of these fields does any one sector have a clear advantage in terms of
    performance

*   risk – handling downside risks, including not only the risk of failing
    to achieve targets but also other risks, e.g. political risk (if some of
    the interventions are overruled by elected politicians).

Social impact bonds are a means of valorising social impact. Government
agrees to pay for measurable outcomes of social projects, and this prospective
income can then be used to raise bond financing from commercial, public
or social investors. This would be possible where outcomes are measurable
and lead to tangible public financial savings. They would be crucial instruments
for financing preventative programmes, and, for social projects, bonds
of this kind would be one way to sustain themselves beyond the period
of initial grants.

# 15 CROWD FUNDING

The age of We-think is already pointing the way to We-Funding. The traditional model has been for the few (banks and other aggregators of capital) to raise finance from the many and fund businesses that sell to the many. Banks are the intermediary institutions that provide the bridge between lending and borrowing. The control of funding is concentrated, whereas saving and consumption are distributed. But the web opens up the possibility of making new types of connection between the many and the many. Where finance can be raised from potential consumers, the distinction between investor and consumer begins to break down.

The Basques have a tradition of Poteo, where a group contribute to
a kitty, elect a treasurer, then tour the tapas bars of the town paid for
by the treasurer out of the kitty. There are similar European traditions
for contributing to leaving presents at work. Could the same idea work
on a larger scale? Could a group buy a football club or even a company?
The problem to date is that the savings from a group are not enough for
large investments. But if there are enough small savers? In February 2008,
26,000 people, responding to a web call, each put £35 into a newly formed
co-op and bought a football club, Ebbsfleet United. Two months later
many of the members – pioneers of a new form of financial collaboration
– travelled to Wembley and saw their side win the FA trophy.

In the past raising cash has either been through a bank or a share issue (in the case of market investment) or through charitable donations (in the case of the grant economy). All these channels are tightly regulated. For social investment projects, as we have seen, a public share issue can cost between £150,000 and £600,000 and take as much as a year to progress through the various hoops that have been put in place over the years to prevent abuses.

With charities it is different. It is the charity which is closely scrutinised, and once approved it can raise funds through campaigns, publicity, and the persuasiveness of its cause. The thinking here is that if people ask for money to benefit others rather than themselves there is much less likelihood of the kind of deception to which an unregulated private market would be prone. As long as an official eye is kept on the accounts and activities of the charity, the appeals for donations need not be scrutinised with the same toothcomb used for a share prospectus.

But this clear distinction between the private investment interest and philanthropic giving is becoming blurred. Social companies may have the same goals and beneficiaries as a charity, but a share issue by a not-for-distributed profit trader is subject to the same complex processes as a private company.

Or a group with a shared interest may want to act collectively as consumers, or workers, or investors in a project. The traditional form here has been a co-operative, but co-operatives, too, are regulated when it comes to investment. A local wind co-operative has to pass through the costly and lengthy process of a prospectus if it wishes to have a share issue, even if, as in Denmark, the investors consume their own energy.

Co-ops are not charities. They act in the interests of their members. But in that they are acting collectively, they are part of the social economy in a way that is distinct both from the private economy, and from charities. For consumers a co-op is a form of collective purchasing. For workers it is a form of collective employment. For all those investing it is a particular form of collective financing and ownership.

## The generosity of crowds

The web gives scope for radical innovations in the sphere of finance. In the grant economy, the cost of fund raising is estimated at 15 per cent to 33 per cent by the US Association of Fundraising Professionals and the Better Business Bureau. Internet donor sites radically reduce this, by providing a platform for fundraisers, lists and assessments of non profits, and lower transactions costs for donations. The US site First Giving, for example, provides a platform and an electronic means of payment that has enabled 1.864 million people to give $100 million to 26,790 non profits, for a basic cost of 7.5 per cent per transaction.[1]

On the First Giving site, issues of trust are addressed by allowing fundraisers to set up their own pages (for a sponsored walk or event for example) which they use to contact their friends. The non profits in question are also required to be registered in another site, Guidestar, that is a not for profit itself committed to increasing transparency in this sector. With 1.7m registered non profits, Guidestar verifies their claims, benchmarks their salaries, and oversees their performance. Sites of this kind act simultaneously as a version of the Charities Commission, as a directory of potential recipients, and an information platform.

We can expect donor sites to develop other features – donor forums, star and/or donor ratings, Good Giving Guides, Amazon-type links ('those who have given to x have also given to y and z') and interactive links between the donors and the not for profits themselves. They promise to change the process of soliciting funds (through viral fundraising), of giving them, and of the continuing relations between the givers and receivers. The relationship of donor or donee is one where there are far reaching possibilities.

In the social economy – where it is not money but impact that is the driver – there is always a problem of tangibility. Normal funding appeals will provide vivid examples of the kind of work undertaken by a charity, but the funds for the most part go into a common pool. Sometimes there is an attempt to earmark the gift for something particular – a child for example, or a goat, but even if they can be earmarked in this way (and the goat has a largely virtual individuality) the post gift relationship is limited.

The web is a means of making this virtual individuality real. Blogs, video connections, and forums allow continuing connections. The act of giving in this case is not the transfer of funds for a good cause, but a gateway to greater engagement. Donating to save a particular area of rainforest, for example, now allows a donor to see exactly how this or that part of the rainforest is progressing. The donation merges into a subscription, and indeed into membership that may carry certain rights such as voting how funds should be used. It provides a micro thread for continuing civic involvement.

## Crowdfunding and politics

It also opens up new forms of political funding and engagement. During the 2004 presidential campaign, Democratic contender Howard Dean used the power of the internet to galvanise grassroots support. Organisations such as

Meetup.com and MoveOn.org were crucial in getting supporters to donate time and money to the campaign. Supporters formed local groups and interacted with Howard Dean on policy and strategy.

The model was developed by Barack Obama, who with Chris Hughes, the co-founder of Facebook, working full-time for him, and others from Silicon Valley, was able to raise vast sums via the internet for the 2008 Presidential election. According to the Federal Electoral Commission, Obama raised $745 million (more than twice his Republican opponent John McCain's total of $347 million). Overwhelmingly, this came in the form of small donations of $200 or less. Indeed, some $335 million was raised this way. More than 80 per cent of individual donations were in donations of $2,000 or less.[2] By the time of his election 3.1 million people had donated to Obama. He had 1.5 million web volunteers, and 8,000 affinity groups supporting his campaign.[3]

## The consumer as investor

When we turn to the market economy, these kinds of innovations are already transforming the way in which investment takes place. New forms of consumer investment are appearing first in the cultural industries. In film, music, sport and journalism, what we call crowdfunding is emerging as a way of allowing those previously seen as consumers to engage in the financing, production and distribution of products or services in which they have an interest. The consumer is being redesignated as a multifaceted fan. Organisations, such as Sell a Band and My Football Club allow fans to invest in projects in return for involvement in the production and management of the project, shared ownership and in some cases a share of future profits.

## SellaBand

SellaBand (sellaband.com), is using crowdfunding as a means of supporting and promoting aspiring artists. It is a German website founded in August 2006, that on the one hand allows artists to create a profile and upload their music, and on the other lets anyone stream the music and if they like it, invest in one or more lots of $10 in an escrow account for a 'part' of a future CD recording. If 5,000 parts are sold, the accumulated $50,000 is released, the band is provided with a recording studio, and an album is produced.

Each owner of a part ('a believer') receives a CD (which they may sell) as well as a share of advertising and revenue from ordinary market sales. All revenues are split three-ways between the artist, the 'believers' and SellaBand. 'Believers' and artists can raise additional revenue by selling the music at concerts, on artists' websites and other retail outlets. As of June 2009, 8,600 bands/artists have used the site to try and raise funds, of which 31 from 13 different countries have sold the necessary 5,000 'parts', and $2.5 million have been invested.

## My Football Club

In the case of records and films, there is a specific product that requires finance and markets. Any investment can be classed as a forward purchase of the product (like membership of a book club) and therefore escape the requirements of a mainstream investment. Purchasing a football club is different. What is on offer here is involvement in the financing, operating and watching a flow of structured inter-connected events.

The idea of My Football Club stemmed from a question about consumption. Why is it, asked its originator, a sporting journalist and advertising copywriter called Will Brooks, that stops us clubbing together to buy things normally only available to the rich – a farm for example, or a radio station? Why does consumption have to remain individual?

One of his interests was football. Why not buy a football club? He launched a website in April 2007 and invited people to subscribe £35 to buy a club. In a little over three months he had 20,000 subscribers and had raised £700,000. Myfootballclub.com was formally established in August 2007. It was immediately approached by a number of professional clubs, and decided (by ballot) to buy and manage Ebbsfleet United, a football club in England's Blue Square Premier League.

There are three key features of this financing. First, My Football Club is a co-op, operating according to one member one vote. £35 is the annual fee to become a member. Second its Articles specify that there will be no distributed profits – this was necessary to avoid the hoops otherwise required by the Financial Services Authority. Third, the members in this case have the right to be actively involved in the running of the club, from the price of tickets, to team selection, player transfers, the player wage limits, even the choice of manager.

The striking thing is that only 1,200 of the 31,500 members are local supporters. 3,000 live in the US, 900 in Australia. In all there are members in 130 countries. They are linked together by an interactive website, serviced by a team of six full timers, with active hosting by a committee of seven (elected initially from 104 nominees). The site's forums receive 25,000 postings a month. Any proposal with 150 supporters can be put to a vote, and to date over 100 votes have taken place. The site is redefining the experience of ownership.

## Crowdfunding and the social economy

In the case of the grant economy web based funding lowers the cost and transforms the flow of information between the two parties of the traditional grant economy – donor and project. In the case of these cultural industry initiatives – all of them operating the private market economy – the connection of investor and consumer in many ways removes them from the market. They still have to hire studios, have CDs cut, and pay footballers. They may sell their surplus CDs on the market, and charge spectators to enter their football ground, but the drive in each case is not to earn money (let alone a profit). It is rather to advance an enthusiasm and – in the case of My Football Club – to be involved in the business of running the club.

The web is a path away from the categories and relationships of the private market into productive collaboration in the social economy. Once they have established their collaborative crowds (and in all these cases the data base is the spine of the organisation) they are able to raise further funds cheaply and rapidly. CTM, the Italian consortia of 130 fair trade consumer co-ops, was able to raise €10m in a month by circulating the 21,000 associated members. The form of financing here is like that found in the household economy – where groups or clubs or networks agree together to contribute to a kitty for a common cause.

Already websites are emerging that provide a platform for this kind of group funding. The UK-based Pledgebank allows people to make a pledge if a certain number of others act likewise by a given date. The pledge might be to use a new rural bus service, to help out at a festival, or to start a community newspaper. But it may also be a straightforward financial pledge. A member of My Football Club who described himself as joint owner of Ebbsfleet United pledged to contribute £20 towards the cost of a new striker for the club if another 1,000 did so by the 21st June 2008. Another 1,000 did and a new striker was bought.

Funding 2.0 is still in its infancy. The examples we have given are less than three years old. But they point in directions of great potential for the expansion of the social economy. If 20,000 people can buy a football club, why can they not establish a fair trade company or buy houses for the homeless? In these cases, as with any project which is not a one off, the challenge is how to keep the communities together. Just as they can form quickly, they can as quickly disband.

The challenge for My Football Club is how to make the experience of ownership rewarding enough for people to renew their membership. The quality of the website, of its forums and of the votes that take place are the things that will decide whether membership is sustained. But if it succeeds then the Ebbsfleet Pioneers will have created a new form of 21st century co-operative, a co-operative of enthusiasts, which, like the Rochdale Pioneers before them, represents a radical innovation in finance and the practice of corporate and community governance.

The web has opened up radically new ways of raising finance, and of connecting those who invest with the projects they fund. Instead of a relationship mediated through a window of numbers – share prices and annual accounts – there is for social investors the possibility of direct relations, of qualitative engagement, and for the projects themselves the possibility of connecting to investors in ways that extend far beyond finance.

References

Benkler, Yochai, 'The Wealth of Networks: How social production transforms markets and freedom', New Haven, Yale University Press, 2006. Available at: http://www.benkler.org/Benkler_Wealth_Of_Networks.pdf

Links
www.meetup.com
www.moveon.org
www.myfootballclub.co.uk
www.fundable.org
www.sellaband.com
www.crowdfunding.pbwiki.com

End notes
1   Sourced on 27th June 2009. Available at: http://www.firstgiving.com.
2   Federal Election Commission. Sourced on June 15th 2009. Available at: http://www.fec.gov/DisclosureSearch/mapApp.do?cand_id=P80003338&searchType=&searchSQLType=&seah Keyword.
3   On Obama's connection to Silicon Valley and the social networking character of his campaign see Joshua Green, "The Amazing Money Machine" in The Atlantic, June 2008.,www.theatlantic.com/doc/200806/obama-finance.

# **16** THE GRANT ECONOMY

Grants are a gift, and on the face of it should be a preferred source of funding. It is free money, without obligation save to use the money for the purpose it was requested. But like all gift relationships, the grant relationship is complex, involving issues of preferment, continuity, obligations and assessment.

In the 1980s the Greater London Council (GLC) controversially pioneered a programme of shifting resources from municipal services to civil society. It launched major funding programmes for the Community Sector, for Arts and the Cultural Industries, for Industry and Employment, Equalities and Health, and for groups working in Housing, Social Services, Planning, the Environment. Most of these programmes were administered by those recruited from the sectors, and they led to a major extension of the network of social organisations in the capital.

By 1985, the programme had reached £80 million, one tenth of the Council's total budget. In 1986 the GLC was abolished, and responsibility shifted to a joint grants funding body run by the London Boroughs. It was then that the fragility of a purely grant-based organisation was highlighted. The grants budget was cut by two-thirds to £26 million, leading to the retrenchment and collapse of many of the newly expanded organisations.

Today, of the 171,000 general charities in the UK, 25,000 receive 75 per cent or more of their income from statutory sources, and are particularly vulnerable to fluctuations in public finance and political and administrative shifts of policy.

We would expect those receiving grants to be unequivocally grateful to the givers of grants – but in surveys of grant programmes in many different countries, there are common dissatisfactions even resentments among the recipients. For example, a survey on grant giving in Australia reported that the grant aided organisations had the following concerns:

- there was a lack of stable and sustainable funds

- the majority of grants were short term and directed away from operational costs, making long term planning difficult

- the cost associated with securing funds was high, with senior management focusing on obtaining funds and spending less time on managing their organisations

- smaller voluntary and community organisations were paying disproportionately high prices for their basic services and overheads.

These problems – that grants were insufficient, unreliable, short term, costly to apply for – at times appear endemic to the grant economy. Similar concerns were expressed in surveys in Canada and France, and are often voiced from our experience in the UK. There are exceptions, but the themes were common enough for those planning to fund their projects over the long term through grant funding to understand what grant receiving may involve. There is in short no such thing as a free grant.

## Structures of giving

There are four characteristics we want to highlight about the grant economy:

i)  **The grant relationship**. Grant giving (and receiving) has at its heart a patron-client relationship, with which neither party is fully at ease. Grant givers (particularly governments) tend to be wary of the obligations entailed in long term commitments and thus limit the length of grants.

Another way grant givers have sought to escape a patron-client relationship (and limit the time frame of support) is to structure their grants round projects and programmes so that grant giving becomes more like the purchase of a project, with a definable package and clearly accountable outcomes and end points. Such a transformation of grants into a quasi market transaction has been a feature of much UK government funding over the past 20 years, reflected in the fact that UK charities have come to rely on an increasing proportion of their income from project funds, and from contracts and sales.

ii)  **Social rather than market valuation of outcomes.** The absence of market measures for grant aided organisations always leaves a central problem as to how to assess impact. It is not that measures and targets cannot be constructed. But it opens up a whole space around the economy of assessment, its mechanisms, costs, and distortions – particularly in fields like caring services where it is the quality of relationships that are central.

iii)  **Cost based finance.** Grants are designed to cover costs. Some of these are tangible like the costs of initial purchases, as well as those for build up and operations. But there is always greater difficulty in finding grants that cover the less tangible items of an enterprise, working capital and risk for example, let alone that contribute to a project's reserves and to a surplus to finance expansion. Some grant funders have committed to the principle of 'full cost recovery' – that grants should cover the full costs of an activity. By contrast private sector providers aim to set their prices to cover the value of the activity to the purchaser – enabling them to take profits.

The grant economy, like the state, is one based on costs not accumulation. It is not structured to adequately deal with the problem of risk or that of expanded investment. When it comes to capitalisation and reserves, whereas private finance welcomes an increase in an enterprise's capital funds to underwrite its long term security, grant givers tend to question an applicant for having too great a financial reserve.

Issues of risk and surplus which in a market enterprise are part of the consideration of capital, are transferred in a grant economy into debates about what is a reasonable estimate of costs in a grant application. If a project manages to reduce costs beneath the agreed level, it is often difficult to carry over these savings as surplus in the project's accounts, without it resulting in a reduction of future funding.

Part of the insecurity of grant aided organisations is that grants are about a flow of funds over a given period rather than the financing of a stock of capital to underwrite longer term security. And since the source of funds for grant givers is itself unstable – not least with governments subject to expenditure cuts – there is an insecurity for grant dependent organisations which is distinct in type from the many insecurities faced in the market.

iv) **Ex ante fixing of costs and outcomes.** Grant giving tends to freeze prospective costs and targeted outcomes at the time of the agreement of the grant. Instead of the flow and flexibility of the market, and the pressure to economise costs and maximise benefits, grants rarely embody these continuing pressures. There may be provisions for review. The grant giver may prove open and flexible. But the inherent structure of grant making (as with public finance) is of costs and targeted outcomes that are static for a given time period.

None of the above speaks against seeking funding through grants, but it does call for an understanding of the nature of a grant relationship and the circumstances of the grant givers and for a careful assessment of the place of grants in the business model for establishing an innovation on a sustainable basis.

## Grant strategies

What follows are some of the lessons we have learnt from both administering grants and receiving them, in order to minimise the problems voiced by the Australian recipients and ensure that grants contribute to their fullest extent in the launch of sustainable innovation:

i) **Equity substitutes.** Grants rarely take the form of equity, but some of the functions of equity can be fulfilled by carefully tailored grants. Grant funding can cover:

- fixed assets (buildings, equipment) which have a longer life than the grant term

- working capital (if in no other way than the up front payment of an annual grant and its investment to provide for a working capital fund)

- build up costs to cover early stage learning, reflected in the level of costs and the establishment of an independently sustainable business model

- contributions in kind – for example low cost premises.

In rare instances quasi equity grants are given. Far sighted government programmes have forward-funded organisations with de facto equity to establish their roots so that they could survive a downturn in public funding. The Hunter Foundation provided finance for fair trade farmers to purchase their equity share of a UK-based fair trade company (an option that other grant programmes should consider). Prizes in competitions are in effect a form of equity for the winners.

ii) **Support packages.** Grants should be approached not just for their finance, but for the networks and support that accompany them. Venture capital and venture philanthropy (**method 17**) offer instructive parallels. Venture capital will normally offer a range of technical support to the firms they back, and link them into other firms in their portfolio.

The best grant programmes and intermediaries follow something of the same model – particularly where they are funding a group of similar initiatives. They can assume a role of the facilitators of collective services, encouraging the sharing of overheads by small start-ups, the sharing of experience and of financial and administrative systems.

iii) **Mutual learning.** Recasting the relationship as one of mutual learning partially erodes the patron-client pairing for it underlines the fact that the grant givers also have interests which they are furthering through those that they fund. For these reasons it is important to choose the donor as carefully as the funders choose the grant recipients. Many of the best programmes are administered by those with experience of operating in the relevant sector, and respected by their peers.

iv) **Three parties not two.** The grant relationship is a three-fold one, between the donor, the recipient, and the beneficiaries. The grant recipient has a critical role in enabling tangible relations between donors and beneficiaries. This is particularly the case where the quality of a grant funded service is difficult to capture in metrics and reports.

v) **Continuity.** One of the problems in establishing strong donor-recipient relations particularly with government funding is that the funding personnel tend to change more rapidly than the personnel they fund. For larger grants, as with public contracts, there is a case for establishing an independent oversight panel to act both as advisors and guarantors of the spirit and integrity of the grant relationship, even when personnel change.

vi) **Wider support.** The vulnerability of a grant funded project to the cycles of state funding and political control can be reduced by establishing a strong basis of support amongst the beneficiaries and contributors to a service. A long established recycling scheme in Colorado developed a system of street recycling representatives that not only acted as a two way contact point for the service, but on four occasions has been a successful mobiliser of mass public opposition to the municipal proposals to axe the service.

vii) **Leveraging networks.** If one of the principles is to develop a wide core of small supporters, then particularly valuable partners are those national voluntary organisations with their own network of individual donors and volunteers. The web too provides a platform for these connections and a means for building up a supporter base of its own. Investment in an interactive and hosted website has become a core requirement for projects in the contemporary social economy.

viii) **Metrics and assessment.** The project should develop together with the beneficiaries its own systems of data gathering and measurement whose primary function is to assist the performance of the service. The results can then be provided to donors and avoid what we call 'alienated metrics' – namely measures imposed from above which are experienced as partial or intrusive, and in some cases may undermine the service.

A project to promote physical exercise on an estate in Kent in the UK found that a range of measures designed to record the impact of the service (weight, health checks, regularity and length of exercise) were experienced as intrusive and would have led to the withdrawal of participation. Instead a simple qualitative 1-5 self assessment was designed, (for example how you are sleeping, levels of energy, and so on) and filled in monthly which gave the participants a sense of their own progress, through a system under their control. At the same time the metrics could be used to report to the County Council funders of the programme, and in turn for their reporting to the Treasury nationally.

ix) **Step by step.** Just as market start-ups run the danger of growing too quickly, so new grant funded social ventures need the speed of the prototyper and the patience of a gardener to grow step by step following the Grameen principle.

x)  **Multiple income streams.** It is clearly wise to diversify the sources of grant funding, yet this runs the danger of diluting the quality of the time that a project can devote to each. A business model for a non market service or project needs above all to find some way of tapping independent income streams that reflect the success of the project. A common experience was that of a successful youth club on a poor housing estate in Salford, which suddenly collapsed through the axing of the public programme that financed it. What is needed in such cases is some form of sister enterprise linked in to the grant funded activity.

Grant funding is valuable in the prototyping and start-up phases of social innovation, but is not a reliable source of long term funding. It can also play an important role as a supplementary funding stream for some of the social elements of social enterprise. The best grants programmes are not merely transfers of finance, but connect new ventures into networks of interested supporters and practitioners. They are less providers of gifts but collaborations.

References
Louisa Thomson and Julie Caulier-Grice, Improving Small Scale Grant Funding for Local, Voluntary and Community Organisations, Young Foundation July 2007

NCVO The UK Civil Society Almanac 2009

End notes
See for example, http://www.nonprofitaustralia.org.au/

# 17 VENTURE PHILANTHROPY

Traditional grant making organisations have for some time been criticised for failing to help non-profits build capacity, grow and become financially sustainable. Venture philanthropy is a response to this criticism, and seeks to use many of the tools of venture capital funding to promote start-up, growth and risk taking social ventures.

At Dialogue Museum guests are led through a series of ordinary situations in total darkness by a blind guide. Without eyesight these 'ordinary' situations become extraordinary. Guests have to rely on other senses to negotiate the obstacles of the everyday. After visiting this exhibition – Dialogue in the Dark – guests can have 'dinner in the dark' where blind waiters serve guests in total darkness.

Dialogue in the Dark is the brainchild of Andreas Heinecke, a social entrepreneur who has for some two decades been tackling issues of disability and marginalisation. Heinecke established Dialogue Social Enteprise which has franchised out a number of initiatives including Dialogue Museum, and Dialogue in Silence – where deaf people provide an insight into non-verbal communication. Dialogue Social Enterprise and its associated franchisees have to date had exhibitions in 25 countries, with over six million visitors worldwide and employed over 6,000 blind or visually impaired people.

Dialogue Museum was supported by Munich based BonVenture, a venture philanthropy organisation which funds commercial and non-profit organisations with a social, ethical or environmental purpose in Germany, Austria and Switzerland. BonVenture provides performance based finance and strategic support to help start-up and grow social purpose organisations. Key objectives are social impact and financial sustainability. BonVenture aims to invest €100,000 – €750,000 per project, together with co-investors, through equity, mezzanine financing, and loans and also provides non-financial services and support through its networks.[1] BonVenture expects Dialogue Museum to generate an annual income of about €500,000 and 50,000 to 80,000 visitors each year.[2]

The term 'venture philanthropy' was first coined in 1969 by John D. Rockefeller III who used it to describe 'an adventurous approach to funding unpopular social causes'. When the term resurfaced in the mid 1990s, it was associated with a growing community of dotcom millionaires who were seeking to apply both their wealth and their business acumen to the most pressing social problems.

The way in which the first venture philanthropists sought to transform the charitable sector alienated many of those they were trying to help. The main elements of venture philanthropy – building operating capacity, close engagement between donors and recipients, and clear performance expectations – were said to be long-standing features of the best philanthropy and not new at all.[3] Yet as the novelty and controversy subsided it was clear that this approach did address some of the limitations faced by many of those operating as donors and recipients in the grant economy.

## Definitions

There are six main features of venture philanthropy as it has come to be practised:[4]

1.  **High engagement:** venture philanthropists have a close hands-on relationship with the social entrepreneurs and ventures they support, driving innovative and scalable models of social change. Some may take board places on these organisations, and all are far more intimately involved at strategic and operational levels than are traditional non-profit funders.

2.  **Tailored financing:** as in venture capital, venture philanthropists take an investment approach to determine the most appropriate financing for each organisation. Depending on their own missions and the ventures they choose to support, venture philanthropists can operate across the spectrum of investment returns. Some offer non-returnable grants (and thus accept a purely social return), while others use loan, mezzanine or quasi-equity finance (thus blending risk-adjusted financial and social returns).

3.  **Multi-year support:** venture philanthropists provide substantial and sustained financial support to a limited number of organisations. Support typically lasts at least three to five years, with an objective of helping the organisation to become financially self-sustaining by the end of the funding period.

4. **Non-financial support:** in addition to financial support, venture philanthropists provide value-added services such as strategic planning, marketing and communications, executive coaching, human resource advice and access to other networks and potential funders.

5. **Organisational capacity-building:** venture philanthropists focus on building the operational capacity and long-term viability of the organisations in their portfolios, rather than funding individual projects or programmes. They recognize the importance of funding core operating costs to help these organisations achieve greater social impact and operational efficiency.

6. **Performance measurement:** venture philanthropy investment is performance-based, placing emphasis on good business planning, measurable outcomes, achievement of milestones, and high levels of financial accountability.

While most American venture philanthropy activity is based on grant making, the Europeans have tended to make use of a broader range of financial instruments and packages that go well beyond simple grants. These include underwriting, mezzanine funding, long-term 'patient' capital as well as equity and 'equity-like' investments and loans.

As such, the defining characteristic of venture philanthropy is not the type of financial package used, but rather, the kind of relationship between the recipient and donor/investor. Far from seeking a financial return on investment as the primary driver, the overwhelming majority of venture philanthropy activity in the US is based on non-returnable grants. In Europe, it is also the case that the social trumps the financial in terms of returns on investment.

Venture philanthropists work with a range of organisations – not solely charities and not for profits. These include social enterprises and social entrepreneurs, trading charities and socially driven commercial organisations.

There are now some 100 venture philanthropy organisations around the world. Just over half are based in the US, a third are European and the rest from elsewhere, reaching as far as Japan, China and Argentina. Originally led by 'high net-worth' individuals and their foundations, it now takes in traditional foundations, hybrid foundations, a range of social venture and ethical funds and even some for-profit funds. Some refer to themselves as primary practitioners who provide financial and non-financial support. These include

BonVenture in Germany, Impetus Trust, CAN-Breakthrough and Venture Partnership Foundation in the UK, d.o.b. Foundation in the Netherlands, Good Deed Foundation in Estonia, Invest for Children in Spain, Oltre Venture in Italy and Social Venture Partners and Venture Philanthropy Partners in the US. There are also a range of organisations – such as UnLtd and Ashoka – which provide either capital or professional services to an organisation – but not both.

For example, CAN-Breakthrough – based in London – provides performance based finance and strategic support to help social purpose organisations scale their social impact. Unlike other venture philanthropists, however, Breakthrough do not provide funding for start-ups and focus instead on providing growth capital to established social enterprises – usually those with at least three years trading history and a sustainable and scalable business model.[5] At the 2007 Charity Awards, Breakthrough were highly commended in the grant making category for 'achieving a breakthrough for social enterprise'.[6]

## Benefits

Since the beginning of the decade venture philanthropy has played an important role in diversifying capital markets for social purpose organisations and reaffirming some key principles for good grant making. In particular they have filled a gap between traditional grants for non profits and commercial market rate equity and loans.[7] Capital investments made by venture philanthropists also aim to address issues of sustainability and scale.

Those seeking funds from venture philanthropists can expect help in strengthening their capacity and management. They often provide skills and expertise that small organisations cannot afford. The funding on offer is usually longer term and takes account of core operations. But above all it is the approach that is distinct. The key word is venturing, with its focus on drive, flexibility, capacity, and all the creativity that is needed for a start up venture to succeed. Far from minimising risk and distancing themselves from operations, venture philanthropists readily shoulder some of the risk and responsibility for success of the venture, and are quite prepared to get engaged and play a role on the board.

### To consider...

Yet there is an issue of contrasting cultures. Social enterprises and grant-based organisations are often highly entrepreneurial, but see through different lenses to those coming from the venture capital (VC) field. VC ideas like performance outcomes, investor control, the bottom line, scaling and exit do not sit easily with a community organisation working on a poor estate. What, for example, does an exit strategy look like for a charity providing a service over the long term?

How does it feel for young people at a youth club to know that they are being measured? How does the commitment to user control fit with ideas of investor control? Where does the balance lie between social and financial returns?

Some venture funds are explicit that it is the financial returns that are primary. Bridges Community Ventures, for example, refused 40 applications for social enterprise funding in 2004 for this reason. But this merely underlines the point we made in relation to equity funding: social purpose organisations must be clear about the terms under which they wish to receive funding. They must be careful in their choice of investing partner to ensure that the partner accepts the primacy of the social mission – that in the words of the Mondragon group 'finance remains subordinate to sovereignty'.[8]

There will always remain a tension between financial and social returns on investment. For venture philanthropists the challenge is how to internalise the distinctive culture and economy of mission-driven organisations in order to be able to provide the expertise, the support and the capital that are often so needed. And reciprocally social organisations need to recognise that they too have much to learn from the venturing skills and imagination of the venture capital community.

While the initial excitement and controversy which surrounded venture philanthropy in the US in the mid 1990s has subsided, the movement continues to develop both in North America and in Europe – where it plays an important role in diversifying capital markets for non profits and social purpose organisations. The field is small but maturing and with it a particular set of skills and methods are being developed which have important ramifications for traditional grant making and grant receiving organisations.

References

Emerson, J, Freundlich, T, and Fruchterman, J, (2007), Nothing Ventured, Nothing Gained: addressing the critical gaps in risk-taking capital for social enterprise, Skoll Centre for Social Entrepreneurship Working Paper, Said Business School, University of Oxford, Oxford: UK

John, R, (2006), 'Venture Philanthropy: the evolution of high engagement philanthropy in Europe', Skoll Centre for Social Entrepreneurship Working Paper, Saïd Business School, University of Oxford, Oxford. Available at: http://www.sbs.ox.ac.uk/NR/rdonlyres/8792299F-F526-4ABE-BE8B-BF7E989A10AC/2079/27200_A_Venture_Philanthropy1.pdf

Milner, A., (eds.) 'European Venture Philanthropy Directory 2008/2009'. Brussels: European Venture Philanthropy Association.

Links

http://www.dialogue-se.com/

End notes

1   Mezzanine finance takes the form of preference shares or subordinated debt, typically unsecured
2   Milner, A., (eds.) 'European Venture Philanthropy Directory 2008/2009': Brussels: European Venture Philanthropy Association. Available at: http://www.evpa.eu.com/downloads/directory/EVPA%20Directory%2008-09_Issue-1.pdf
3   See for example, Letts, C, Ryan, W, and Grossman, A (1997), Virtuous Capital: what foundations can learn from venture capital, Harvard Business Review, Cambridge, MA.
4   See Milner, A., (eds.) 'op cit'.
5   Milner, A., (eds.) 'ibid'.
6   http://www.charityawards.co.uk/home/category.php?cat=7&yr=1
7   Emerson, J, Freundlich, T, and Fruchterman, J, (2007), Nothing Ventured, Nothing Gained: addressing the critical gaps in risk-taking capital for social enterprise, Skoll Centre for Social Entrepreneurship Working Paper, Said Business School, University of Oxford, Oxford: UK
8   Some critics see only the corrosive danger of venture philanthropy for social organisations. They argue that they are oil and water and can never mix. The W.K. Kellogg Foundation recently wrote that "the emphasis on sustainability, efficiency and market share has the potential to endanger the most basic value of the non-profit sector—the availability of 'free space' within society for people to invent solutions to social problems and serve the public good." See also Edwards, M., (2008) 'Just Another Emperor? The Myths and Realities of Philanthrocapitalism', Demos: London. Available at: http://www.justanotheremperor.org/

# SECTION 4: CULTURE, KNOWLEDGE AND RELATIONAL CAPITAL

New ventures put much of their energy into securing financial capital: money to invest in fixed assets on the one hand, and working capital on the other. But relational capital is just as important. This is both the knowledge and trust built up between a venture and its users and suppliers, and the relationships between a venture and its staff and circle of volunteers. Conventional accounting takes little account of this intangible capital, yet in all social ventures it is the foundation of their strength and of their distinctiveness.

Economics talks of human capital, in the sense of the knowledge and skill developed in individuals. Sociologists introduced the notion of social capital in juxtaposition to individual actions mediated by contracts. They used it to describe the value of trust, norms and networks in permitting co-operative action.[1] We use the concept of relational capital, not to distinguish it from the rare and solitary state of a-normal individuals, but to capture the quality of relationships within which economic exchanges take place. This is the issue of greatest relevance for a social venture for it is on the range and depth of its relationships that its fortunes depend.

These relationships are multifaceted. They include the nature of its connections to users and investors, to suppliers and distributors, and with its own staff and Board and volunteers. With many of them there will be formal agreements, but whereas in the private market economy relationships take place across a territory demarcated by the interests and boundaries of private property and contract, for a social venture the boundaries are more porous and internal and external interests mesh.

It is one of its greatest potential assets that a social venture can attract support and resources from outside itself, as well as motivation from within, on the basis of its ideas and the way it works to realise them. This creates particular issues for management. We can speak of the liquid enterprise, where the challenge is how to manage the flow and direction of the currents. In such an enterprise a critical question is the development of a common culture, for that will provide the cohesion to govern these flows.

# 18 KEEPING IT OPEN

In their purpose and structure social ventures have an interest in openness. They can attract generosity from many unexpected quarters – of knowledge, and connections and offers of time. Once established their goal is to spread their service and know-how as widely as possible. Yet the pressures on management are towards that which can be directly managed through contractual relations – towards a certain enclosure. There are moats between paid staff and volunteers, and chasms between internal and external communications. How can it be otherwise? How can the complex relation of social networks and the gift economy become an asset not a threat to an already overstretched staff? How can resources of goodwill be searched out and tapped into without diverting the staff from their daily tasks?

Sekem was founded in 1977 by an Egyptian pharmacologist, Ibrahim Abouleish, to make an oasis in the desert. After drilling for water, he planted trees, then started to grow bio-dynamically, making compost to give substance to the soil. He and his team began with herbal teas and vegetables which they sold on the Egyptian and European markets, and later other herbs. They established food processing plants and a company to make natural pharmaceutical remedies. Sekem markets the products of its own five farms and those of another 300 organic farmers. It has created an organic mark, and a new model for farming practices.

When pesticide residues were found on the vegetables, Abouleish traced them to distant cotton spraying. So he researched organic cotton, pioneered it, then spun it and made it into clothing. These methods spread nation wide, increasing cotton yields by 30 per cent and cutting Egypt's pesticide use by 90 per cent. The profit from these ventures went to fund a kindergarten, a school and a medical centre, vocational training and now a University.

These successive innovations have only been possible because of Abouleish's ability to keep Sekem open – open to ideas and values from different traditions, open to volunteers and a continuous flow of visitors, and to many partners who shared Sekem's goals. He travelled to Europe to look for ideas and people. He gave talks and set up research centres. The idea and its values were the magnet. The projects gave the focus. The open culture he fostered generated the resource.

One of the hardest things for a new venture is to establish a culture of openness. The demands of a start-up are so consuming that staff are forced to focus inwards even though external links – to suppliers and market outlets – are critical. The tendency will be to strip out the inessentials and to limit the number of interactions – to keep it simple since complexity is unmanageable. So the fewer funders and suppliers the better. Small orders or requests appear to be not worth the time that has to be spent on them. A Board may be necessary but staff often experience it as a diversion. And still the day is never long enough.

Yet many of the most successful social ventures have found ways of maintaining that openness. These include:

- involving organisations and individuals with existing strong social networks in the financing and establishment of a new venture (Divine Chocolate has drawn much of its strength from the involvement of Comic Relief, Christian Aid and Gordon and Anita Roddick in its funding and governance)

- through the pioneering evangelism of the founders – often those on the Board, who act as promoters and channels to relevant networks. In time it should be an aim for all staff and those involved in the venture to gain the skills and confidence to make presentations and connect externally. A recent analysis of 12 successful social ventures identified the development of inspiring evangelists as one of the six common features of success[2]

- through the design of a working space which inspires visitors by the tangibility of its values and practicality. Farms like Sekem have an advantage here – they are a natural living museum – as are schools and clinics and workshops. For ventures based in offices, walls can be used to show visually the character and work of the project – with photos and up to date graphs, progress charts and work plans. The office, too, can be thought of as a working museum, with samples and laboratories, and a small reception area with videos and printed material

- to organise events and experiences that are part of the project – a trade fair or exhibition, for example, or a conference and cultural events. Fair trade is often remembered for its dancing – a celebration that crosses language and cultural divides. One of London's community swimming pool campaigns organises an annual street party. Slow Food has communal meals rather than meetings as a focus to draw in and inspire

- to arrange for visits and tours to foster interconnection and 'learning by visiting'

- to have a regular time and space for reflection on progress, involving paid staff and selected colleagues from outside. This should be accompanied in due course with seminars and workshops on wider issues connected to the project, and eventually to academies for study, research and formation (**method 20**)

- to appoint specialist staff or volunteers whose task it is to be the two way ambassadors of the project – responsible for widening awareness of the project, as well as bringing ideas and people back in. Conventionally part of this work is defined as a public relations function, carried out through press releases, the placing of articles, and PR events. But this assumes a 'private' venture speaking to a general 'public', whereas the task is to multiply interconnections within a wider social network. So the posts should be known as Network Relations (NR) rather than PR posts

- to establish from the beginning a web 2.0 presence, with forums and stories, a daily blog and postings of problems for which the venture is searching for solutions and contacts. This is a cultural project of its own, that needs full time hosting to build an audience and attract resources as well as serving as an interface between the internal world of the venture and all those outside

- to modularise the venture into multiple poles, that make their own external connections including open source use of the website. One of the values of open source and intranet methods of developing and managing a project is that it allows senior managers to keep in touch without the formality of meetings and reports.

The point running through all these practices is that social organisations critically depend on a culture. Culture is itself a form of organisation. As such it spills over the dividing lines of ownership, and the lines of organisational charts. It spreads like a cloud, and connects not just through information and its communication – though this is an important part of it – but through shared experience and the participation in a common project.

Many of the structures that have sought to make external connections – such as Boards, and memberships, and affiliates to a project – have too often been insufficient on their own. They are time consuming for any venture to organise and tend not to rank high in the table of priorities. But these more open forms offer a way of giving substance to these forms, and in doing so strengthen the mechanisms of governance.

Investing in the human resources to ensure a social venture's openness is as important as investing in a building or a machine. For it concerns the formulation and presentation of a venture's identity, to itself and to the outside world. The quality and extent of a project's external relationships should be thought of as a cultural project, for it is from an open and inclusive culture that a social venture draws much of its strength.

References
Ibrahim Abouleish, Sekem: a Sustainable Community in the Desert, Floris, 2004

End notes
1  See James Coleman, Foundations of Social Theory, Harvard University Press, 1990 pp 300-321, and Robert Putnam, Making Democracy Work, Princeton University Press, 1994, Chapter 6.
2  Leslie Crutchfield and Heather McLeod, Forces for Good: the Six Practices of High Impact Nonprofits, Jossey Bass 2007. The other five were nurturing non profit networks, sharing leadership, smart adaptability, using markets, and linking service and advocacy.

# 19 INTELLECTUAL PROPERTY

A key area for openness is a venture's knowledge and skills. Growth, innovation and impact are all strengthened by open access to knowledge and information. How then should a social venture deal with the know-how it develops? What kind of intellectual property and what level of openness are appropriate for such a venture?

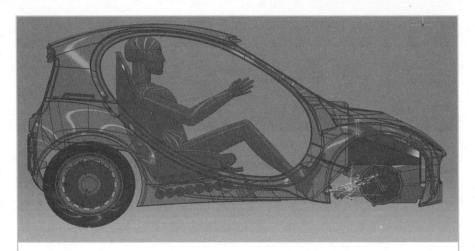

Who will build the car of the future? General Motors in the States? Toyota in Japan? Or a newer firm from India or China? Riversimple, a UK-based transport company, believes that the answer lies not with a single company working on its own but in harnessing the knowledge and ideas of a global community of volunteers, engineers, students and small manufacturers. They are currently working on the world's first open source eco-car, an urban two-seater (pictured above), powered by hydrogen fuel cells.

The car has been designed to achieve the equivalent of over 280 miles per gallon. It can get from 0 to 50 kilometres per hour in 5.5 seconds and has a top speed of 80 kilometres per hour. The car weighs 350 kilograms, roughly half the weight – and therefore more fuel efficient – than its competitors the G-Whiz and Smart cars. The car is also designed to be recycled. It was launched in London in June 2009.

In the information age, IP (intellectual property) has become a central part of business models. Protecting it has become one of the factors that force commercial firms to close themselves off behind castle walls of confidentiality, and to hunt down those who breach the virtual defences of the patent, the trademark and the copyright.

In the social economy things are not so straightforward. Rather than restricting access to their knowledge and information, social ventures have an interest in diffusing and sharing them with others in the social economy. Once the costs of generating information are paid, there is a strong economic case for circulating it for free. This is not only the case in the short run, but in the long term information distributed at its marginal cost provides a cheap input for the future.

In The Human Genome Project for example, companies, public bodies and individual researchers all shared data and as a result, mapped the genome much more quickly than any individual attempt could have done. It underlines the point that restricted circulation of information today, limits the production of information tomorrow. Pricing information or limiting access immediately reduces its spread.[1]

The social economy therefore has an inherent interest in open information systems. Yet for a social venture this reduces the potential income it can earn from its intellectual assets and skills. How then can social innovators recoup their investment and generate new intellectual assets in the future?

## How to keep it open

There is a balance to be struck between covering past costs and future investment and maximising the venture's social contribution. But in an increasing number of cases, notably in software, environmental technologies, medical sciences and genetics, the social benefits of sharing information and 'keeping it open' will outweigh the financial benefits of any potential income from the sale of intellectual property.

The first point is one of reciprocity. If a venture contributes its information openly, then others will be open back. There will always be 'free riders' – those who take but do not give back, but there are ways in which this free ridership can be limited. As with common land prior to the enclosure movement, there were strict rules of use and access to prevent over-grazing.[2]

Second, rather than charging for access to particular information, social ventures can generate income in other ways. As we showed in **method 2**, they can monetise the value of the audience, raising revenue from advertising or even (and within parameters) selling information on site users. They can generate voluntary subscriptions, or where there is a defined community of benefit, as in the case of the electric car, then there is the potential for consortia finance. Some universities in the US collect regular fees from students to donate to creators whose work can be downloaded.

Grant funders, who have an interest in widening impact, are natural allies (and funders) for a venture that pursues an open information policy. There is also the potential for income earning linked to bespoke adaptations of the information – advisory consultancies for example, or the development of applications. In this case the venture is valorising its capacity based on its participation in the reciprocal economy of information.

Third, there are reputational economies, for we see an open information policy as one means of strengthening external relationships – what we have called relational capital – particularly relevant for those organisations (in the development field for example) who would in any case earn little from IP.

## Open models of production

As the engineers from Riversimple emphasise, in an era when information is at the heart of production and innovation, collaboration is as important as competition. This is clearest in the open source software movement and developments such as the Linux operating system, the Mozilla Firefox browser and the Apache web server. These forms of production are now permeating other areas of the social and informational economies. As well as Riversimple's open source eco-car there are open source houses, open source wind turbines, open source heating systems and so on.

Such open and collaborative forms of production are inherently social. They are non-market and non-proprietary. They are in direct contrast to traditional industries which in recent decades, have successfully pressed for property rights to be extended to cover business methods, databases, software and areas of biotechnology. As we have seen even colours, names, plants and seeds can be 'owned'. Yet this tightening of IP has taken place at a time when the internet has made it easier and cheaper than ever before to exchange, copy and distribute information. This is one of the central tensions of the contemporary economy. It is a tension between the old economy and the new, and in this field the social economy is very much part of the new.[3]

## Propertising rather than privatising

If the future is the commons, the question is how it is to be managed. A valuable distinction has been made between propertising and privatising. Propertising is establishing rights over information and the terms on which it can be used. It introduces the idea of degrees of openness, and of means to strengthen a reciprocal economy by limiting free riders.

Increasingly, online contracts, click wrap agreements and so on are being used to outline terms and conditions of use. This is one approach. Another is to use licences to permit certain re-uses.

Unlike traditional copyright which restricts the rights of users, open licences, with 'all rights reversed', enable people to use, copy, amend and distribute material with little or no restriction.[4] Examples include: the Creative Commons, Free Documentation and Open Publication Licenses. Essentially, these licences create a freely accessible 'commons' of information with some rights for authors and creators.

Open licensing has redrawn the traditional battle lines between the interests of society and the interests of individual creators: it enables broader access to information while providing incentives to creators by enabling them to retain some rights over their works.

The first open licence was the General Public License, developed by Richard Stallman in the early 1980s. Stallman opposed proprietary software as undermining the collaborative spirit that had previously characterised the programming community. When he started to develop the GNU operating system in 1983, he decided to license it under the General Public License to allow people to use the program, copy it, make amendments and distribute modified versions. The GPL remains one of the better known and used software licences but it has also helped spawn a series of others – including the Intel Open Source License and the Berkeley Software Distribution licences which are even less restrictive.[5]

Creative Commons licences can be used beyond software. They can be applied to anything that is protected by copyright – this includes books, blogs, photographs, films, songs and so on.[6] Creative Commons has four 'baseline rights'[7]: attribution (by), share-alike (sa), no-derivative works (nd), non commercial (nc). Authors and creators can choose any of these, or combinations, to form the basis of their licence. An author, for example, can choose a by-sa licence which would enable users to distribute and reproduce works as long as they attributed the author and 'share alike' or share back the results of what they do with the work.

Creative commons and other open licences are providing a new model for access to knowledge and information. They are helping to create a pool of information which is freely accessible, maintaining attribution and recognition, while granting authors greater flexibility to determine how their works are going to be used.[8]

Social ventures have an interest in adopting open forms of intellectual property. They stand to benefit from a shared commons of knowledge, both in what they receive back from a reciprocal economy of information, and in extending the value and impact of the knowledge they contribute. Open licensing allows people to build on a venture's knowledge assets and to mix together its assets with others. For some ventures this may involve the foregoing of possible income streams from the sale of that knowledge, but there are many alternative means of generating income, not least through the strengthening of the venture's relational capital through a policy of open information.

External Links
Open Knowledge Foundation – http://www.okfn.org/
Creative Commons – www.creativecommons.org
Free Software Foundation – www.www.fsf.org
Open Source Initiative – www.opensource.org
GNU Operating System – www.gnu.org

References
Moore, Gale, 'The Phenomenon of Openness', idea&s: the arts & science review 4 (2): 28-32, 2007. Available at: http://www.ideasmag.artsci.utoronto.ca/issue4_2/moore.pdf
Landes, William & Richard Posner, 'An Economic Analysis of Copyright Law', Journal of Legal Studies vol. 18, issue 2, 1989, pages 325-63. University of Chicago Press.
Richter, Wolf, (2008) 'Intellectual property law and the performance of distributed problem solving networks (DPSN)', Oxford. Part of the Oxford Internet Institute study on the performance of distributed problem solving networks. Available at: www.oii.ox.ac.uk/research/project.cfm?id=45
Steven Weber, The Success of Open Source, Harvard University Press, 2004

End notes

1   Arrow, K., (1959) 'Economic welfare and the allocation of resources for invention', Santa Monica: RAND. Available at www.rand.org/pubs/papers/2006/P1856.pdf See also Benkler, Y., (2006), 'The Wealth of Networks: how social production transforms markets and freedom', Yale University Press.

2   For a discussion of the first enclosure movement and parallels to the current 'enclosure' of information and other modern 'commons' see Peter Barnes, Capitalism 3.0, Berrett Koehler, 2006 available on line at http://www.capitalism3.com/files/Capitalism_3.0_Peter_Barnes.pdf. As he points out the real danger to commons was enclosure and trespass by outsiders.

3   Some organisations have developed new business models without recourse to greater protection through new pricing models such as iTunes, Spotify, mixcloud or Last.fm. Most, however, have sought to strengthen their intellectual property rights and the means of enforcing them through, for example, Digital Rights Management and lobbying government for copyright term extensions for sound recordings.

4   For a definition see: http://www.opendefinition.org/; http://www.gnu.org/philosophy/free-sw. html; http://www.opensource.org/docs/definition.php.

5   For a list, see http://www.opensource.org/licenses/alphabetical.

6   http://wiki.creativecommons.org/Before_Licensing.

7   These baseline rights are: Attribution. You let others copy, distribute, display, and perform your copyrighted work – and derivative works based upon it – but only if they give credit the way you request. Non-commercial. You let others copy, distribute, display, and perform your work – and derivative works based upon it – but for non-commercial purposes only. No Derivative Works. You let others copy, distribute, display, and perform only verbatim copies of your work, not derivative works based upon it. Share Alike. You allow others to distribute derivative works only under a licence identical to the licence that governs your work. See http://creativecommons.org/about/licence/.

8   An increasing number of social ventures such as mySociety, Akvo, and Tactical Tech have now adopted open licences for these reasons.

# 20 FORMATION: DEVELOPING SKILLS AND CULTURES

Formation is a French word (similar to the German Bildung) for which there is no precise English equivalent. It indicates both personal development (new knowledge, experience and a broadening and deepening of skills) and the development of a shared culture. For a new venture, it underpins the central idea, and informs all its practice.

Niagara Peninsula Homes (NPH) is a Canadian housing co-op that develops and supports 44 co-operative housing projects with 2,000 dwellings in Ontario. Like many of the 2,200 housing co-ops in Canada it is run predominantly by women, and geared to the needs of those on low incomes, particularly single parent families, those with disabilities, new Canadians, and First Nations aboriginal people. The co-op members (including those with severe disabilities) contribute to the upkeep, childcare, and administration of the co-op. Overall there are 90,000 co-op dwellings in Canada valued at C$5.7 billion.

The key to the housing co-ops is the programme of training and formation – in the principles and practice of co-operative living and management, as well as the processes of housing development, finance and administration. These programmes that take place at every level of the co-operative housing movement provide the unifying ethic and the necessary technical, organisational and entrepreneurial skills.

Apart from its housing, NPH launched a good food box scheme for 700 households, and ran nutrition education programmes to support healthier eating. They established a Women's Enterprise Centre, and vocational and business development courses for women. This led to a project that created 50 new food products and a Niagara food basket marketed to hotels and tourists. Later they took over an industrial kitchen that now makes 'own label' products for local food firms. Through all these projects and their numerous training programmes runs a common ethic of mutual help and social justice.

Many of the most successful social ventures have sprung from traditional institutions that for ideological reasons have formation as a primary principle – churches, co-operatives, the military and trade unions are all examples. In faith-based organisations, there is not only the unifying bond of the faith and its practices, but also a recognition of the importance of continuing education and training for the effectiveness of the project. Such organisations can therefore make extensive use of volunteers without compromising their organisation's integrity. It is notable that many social innovators have themselves been formed through religious organisations.[1]

The co-operative movement is another example – not just in the Canadian housing case – but throughout the network. In the UK the Co-op College is responsible for providing courses, but also now a wide range of materials for use within particular co-operative organisations. The Mondragon Group of Co-operatives emerged in the 1950s out of a cultural and educational process. Its progenitor, the parish priest Jose Maria Arizmendiarrieta, founded a Professional School in 1945 which later became the Mondragon University.

In some cases the educational initiative is a place for gathering together the specialist knowledge of social movements, and of forming activists to diffuse the work of that movement. Forum for the Future is an example in the environmental field, or the University of Gastronomy established in Bra, Northern Italy by the Slow Food movement. The Vocational College and the University of the Sekem project in Egypt prepares students with the outlook and skills for promoting bio-dynamic agriculture and other aspects of anthroposophical living.

In other instances, a college or course becomes the channel for generating new projects as well as supporting existing ones. This is the case with the Barefoot College which has been the organising hub for work with the very poor in Rajasthan. Or it is a practice for enabling reflection on the work being undertaken, and in doing so developing a common ethic and approach to these issues. This was the case with the Centro Studi and the methods of Danilo Dolci in Sicily.[2]

It is a feature of sustained social ventures that they have developed spaces, informal or formal, in which a process of formation takes place. Indeed if a venture lacks such a space it is likely to be a critical weakness, equivalent to lacking a proper system of financial accounting.

The importance of a process of formation for new ventures is four-fold:

- it provides a way for everyone involved in the project to develop a shared and articulated aesthetic. In terms of 17th century religion, it internalises the spirit within each person rather than having it laid down by a privileged hierarchy of priests. In organisational terms, it does away with one of the functions of line managers

- it is a platform for reflexivity, away from the tyranny of the immediate. It gives the chance for everyone to stand back and think through the problems of the venture's development as they arise. As such it promotes distributed innovation

- it is a way of developing and refining the general idea in the light of the practice, so that the mission becomes dynamic rather than an abstraction that does not inform the work of the venture

- it helps keep the venture open rather than closed (**method 18**) allowing those who are volunteers and well wishers as well as board members to meet and engage in the reflexive life of the company. This may be as teachers, or as course participants.

New ventures should consider how this function is to be fulfilled from the start. It can be formal or informal. It is useful to assign specific responsibility and resources for developing this function, and consider how it can be used to strengthen the venture's governance (**method 10**).

For social ventures formation plays the integrating role that self-interest plays in utilitarian market theory. It informs the articulation of the central purpose of the venture. It provides meaning for those working for the venture, and for investors and volunteers. It gives to the venture a living, reflexive power that is not limited to particular individuals or levels in the organisation but to all those involved.

End notes

1 Andrew Mawson of the Bromley-by-Bow Centre was a Minister in the United Reform Church, and the two chief executives who succeeded him were also church members. Many of the social economy innovators in Latin America and Africa have been priests and ministers. For a church where volunteers played the role of lay teachers see the interview with Father Leo Bartel in Peter Drucker, Managing the Non Profit Organisation, Collins 1990 pp 161-169.

2 The industrial districts of small and medium enterprises in the Third Italy like the furniture districts in Jutland have technical colleges at the heart of their local economies. Producers meet there and contribute to teaching a new generation, reproducing relationships and skills which underpins the resilient networks of these networked industrial systems. There are similarities with the 70 or so Land Grant Colleges in the US, set up in the second half of the 19th century, to form a productive class of farmers and small miners. They had attached to them agricultural experimental stations which together with a network of specialist county agents, provided a support structure for the farmers.

# 21 USERS AT THE CENTRE

'Start with the users' has been the guiding principle for public service innovation and the principle is a good starting point for social innovation more generally. Users should remain a continuous reference point once the service is in place. If service is seen as a continuing process rather than a fixed formula, then real time feedback systems between the service and its users will always be central to this process of adaptation.

Early diagnosis is key in preventing the progress of diabetes, but screening is not universal, and many health authorities suspect that demographically they should expect higher rates of diabetes than are reported. This is particularly the case in areas with high Asian and Afro-Caribbean populations which have respectively six times and three times the norm.

In Slough, where 30 per cent of the population are from ethnic minorities, the local PCT engaged Dr Foster, a doctor initiated research company, to apply techniques of commercial market analysis to map the actual and potential incidence of diabetes. They developed a computer programme that linked medical data with residency, age and a host of variables from TV watching and car use, to newspaper reading, occupation and shopping.

This allowed the PCT to target their approaches through particular media to the most susceptible groups of people. They also converted a bus, staffed by volunteers and staff, equipped with testing equipment that went to workplaces, shopping and leisure centres and other areas of high susceptibility. In the first three months there was a 164 per cent increase in early detection of diabetes.

Dr Foster has since applied these techniques to many health issues, such as the use of Experiens mapping to identify breast cancer risk for each PCT, analysing Accident and Emergency attendance, hospital re-admission rates, patient experience and demographic data on such things as smoking, binge drinking, and sexual diseases. All of these involve the use of modern statistical techniques and programmes to improve understanding and links to the user.

Social ventures need to be aware of two occupational hazards in their relation to users. Both derive from what we call the narcissism of the idea. By this we mean that an organisation can become so self absorbed in the ethical virtues of its governing idea that it fails to give sufficient attention to a detailed understanding of the characteristics and responses of its users (or indeed its funders) and how it communicates with them.

For many social ventures the key issue is supply not demand. The problem if anything is what criteria to adopt to determine access to a service (affordable housing for example, or medical care) when need and demand greatly exceed supply. There is particular pressure on the state committed as it is to a universal service with limited resources. Far from promoting the service, the pressure is to find ways of reducing demand. From this perspective, finance and time need to be focussed on expanding supply not analysing demand.

This is one of the reasons why the techniques of the market economy where demand is critical have been so slow to be adopted in the social sphere. Yet innovative public service design demonstrates not only the importance of a deep understanding of the different circumstances and aspirations of users in the design of the service, but the need to design new forms of communication between the user and the service. Instead of forms and 8-minute episodes with a GP or specialist, there are 24 hour contact points using text messaging (in New York General Practice) and (in the case of renal treatment) continuous digital monitoring. There are forums and chat rooms, and personal contact points rather than the impersonal contacts of a call centre.

We know that when some of the techniques of commercial user analysis (such as market segmentation methods) are applied to health and public services they can result in radically improved targetting and access to the services, and to differentiation and fine tuning of the services themselves (Ealing Community Transport used acorn group methods for designing its recycling services for example). They suggest that universal services can become more effective and efficient if they move beyond a mass service model and design their services around the particular rather than an aggregated norm.

There are similar results from services where front line staff and users themselves are closely involved in service design and feedback on delivery. It is one of the strengths of many third sector services that volunteers and front line staff play an important role in the shaping and reshaping of services. Organisations like Age Concern and Help the Aged have a highly distributed network of staff and volunteers to provide their services, and together with online forums, have an informal channel for feedback and suggestions for innovation.

The development of web 2.0 greatly enhances the scope for such feedback and discussion, which is why from the start an actively hosted site should be a feature of all new social ventures. A number of web based social feedback sites are now being developed. Patient Opinion is one example. It was established as a social enterprise by Dr Paul Hodgkin, a Sheffield GP, to provide a platform for those using NHS hospitals to feedback to the providers. Its recent postings have such headlines as: "Unhappy with cleanliness at Derriford A&E," "So good after temporal lobectomy that I'm now helping others", "Waiting 3 weeks for therapy for my pressure sore", "Thank you to Bransholme out of hours district nurses". The success of this site was one of the prompts that led the NHS to include feedback and blogs on its new NHS Choices website, and the two now have a mash-up so that the comments submitted on either can be read on both.[13]

There are similar sites for local authority services, such as Fix My Street, where residents can post issues concerning their street or neighbourhood and the moderators follow it up with the council officials concerned. New York's 311 hotline has become a paradigm in this field. Set up in 2003 with 375 staff and responding to 22,000 calls a day, it allows New Yorkers to call in to report civic problems (there are 7,000 city services), receive a service request number and track progress on response (potholes, missing hydrant covers, noise and so on). The lesson from 311 is that citizens become part of the service in providing feedback on that service (city workers are also encouraged to use the line to report issues they come across in their daily work). As a result, not only is a problem more rapidly resolved (the pothole filled) but the calls are analysed by computer programmes, and patterns observed so that the causes of the problems can be tracked down (the clustering of noise complaints or illegal dumps for example).

There are many parts of the social economy in which the citizen plays a central productive role where similar information systems can dramatically improve the service. To take recycling for example, it is now possible to barcode recycling boxes, weigh the contents, analyse patterns of involvement, and feedback to householders. The feedback may take the form of thanking them for participating, following up with non participants, and providing everyone with the practical and environmental results of the collaborative effort, as well as details about the destination of the recyclate and its uses.

The Japanese industrial system is information intensive. To go into a Japanese plant is to see production information everywhere, collected by the workforce, then analysed and acted on by them. Systems that provide means of accessible, rapid feedback and enable users to play a central role in improving production (from Amazon type rating systems or 311 lines to engaging in problem solving along the lines of Innocentive) provide parallel possibilities in the services of the social economy.

Small social ventures at one level are limited when compared to the 7,000 services of New York city government. But the approach and mind-set should be similar in recognising the importance both of channels of feedback (qualitative and quantitative) and the observation of patterns of response. The increasing cheapness of these information tools – some of which can be downloaded freely from the net – means that they can be included as central building blocks in any new venture.

Social ventures tend to rely on their idea to galvanise funders and users. They place their operational focus more on supply than demand. Demand in terms of need appears so self evident, that it is how to expand supply rather than understand the details of demand that can become paramount. But to ensure that the venture remains generative rather than static, users should remain central – a service should know who they are and who is missing, how the service is used and perceived, how it could be improved and added to. Just as no venture can operate without a finance and accounting system, so it requires a system of user relationships and feedback as part of its operational spine.

Links
www.drfosterintelligence.co.uk/marketingServices/whatWeDo
www.iccs-isac.org/en/isd/cs_new_york_311.htm

# 22 BRANDING

It is hard for any venture not to turn to where the money is. For grant-based organisations it is to donors. For contract suppliers it is to the client managers. For social enterprises it is to markets. With markets the connection between users and income is direct – the buyers pay the price. But in many cases the link between the venture and its users is mediated by others. A social enterprise may find its path to the consumer has to pass through so called category managers and the supermarket itself. Or in the case of a social service, the users do not pay, but their take-up and their views count (or should count) with the service commissioners. Any social venture therefore has to address multiple audiences. In all of them it finds itself competing in an economy of attention.

Cafédirect originated in 1991 from discussions in Mexico between the fair trade organisation Twin Trading and coffee co-operatives whose green coffee Twin Trading had been selling on the London market. They had the idea that the co-ops could earn more if their coffee was sold as a brand, so Twin teamed up with three other fair trade organisations in the UK, Oxfam, Traidcraft and Equal Exchange, each of whom had sales outlets that could sell the new brand.

The first packaging was designed for little money by well wishers. Ad specialists came in after work to help on the launch adverts. The early ads (see left and middle) featured the growers and intentionally contrasted them with the smooth, deracinated models in the Nestlé ads. They emphasised the impact of fair trade for farmers ('You discover excellent coffee. They discover school') and the fact that Cafédirect cut out the middleman.

Later the emphasis switched to the quality of the coffee since it became clear that it was the product quality that was decisive for most purchasers, and the social impact was a bonus. Divine Chocolate chose its name for the same reason rather than Just Chocolate. In the Cafédirect 2003 ad on the right a mountain road in the Peruvian Andes is shown rising like steam from a cup of coffee, with the strap line '5065 The Height of Coffee Taste' referring to the optimum height at which the best coffee is grown.

In addition to advertising, Cafédirect sponsors arts events, and now earns a quarter of its income from cafés and other 'out of home' outlets, which are an additional way of getting attention for the brand. Within a decade of its launch more than 50 per cent of UK consumers recognised the Cafédirect brand.

What were formerly rivers of information have become a torrential flood. Firms, ventures and governments compete furiously for attention ('eyeballs'), as well as affection.[1] Social ventures have somehow to navigate this flood.

We argued earlier that ventures should place users at the centre (**method 21**). But why should users respond? Why should people become users of a service, or buy an ethical product? The question extends beyond users to volunteers and funders. Why should those who have funds to give choose one venture rather than another? How, in other words, can a venture stand out amidst this cacophony of noise and become a pole of attraction?

There will always be some who know the venture well – local projects always have an advantage here – but all ventures face a long tail of anonymity. Branding is the venture's costume that it wears on its journey into this realm of the unrecognised and the unnamed. It has always been so. The Salvation Army was a name and a costume. It was the sound of a brass band on the pavement. In its distinction it echoed its opposite – the military with their name and uniforms. The church has its costumes and emblems, political parties their colours, social movements their signifiers (wrist bands, ribbons, poppies and other buttonholes). All are informational shorthands about what an organisation stands for, about its substance.

Brand is an old English word meaning a burning piece of wood. Every social ventures needs to have its distinguishable flame. It starts with its sticks of wood – the idea, the narrative, and the business model (**method 1**). But it also has to decide on its name.

The economy of attention has generated its own economy of naming. It is an economy that has witnessed an extraordinary recent enclosure of the verbal commons, with the trademarking of words and their licensing as URLs for the web. Liberation Nuts, the fair trade nut company, prepared a shortlist of 50 from a long list of 1,000 names, and of this short list, only two were not taken. There is an ever growing profession of brand specialists and professors of sound who advise on neologisms now that so many daily words have been leased. Advertisers pay crossword enthusiasts with wine and a cheque to play with words and their meaning. These are the poets of the branding era.

Alongside the poets, there are artists, the specialists in form and colour. They are the designers of logos and packaging, of the uniforms worn by products and service providers, from street sweepers to air stewardesses. Form and colour have also become proprietorial. Cadbury for example have trademarked some 80 spectra of the colour purple in connection with the sale of chocolate.

There is form and there is substance. Social ventures for the most part are suspicious of form. They share with philosophers and farmers a commitment to substance, and a belief that substance will speak for itself. This view suggests that just as print and style should not get in the way of the meaning of the writer, so the form in which a social venture presents itself should be transparent and neutral. If there is an aesthetic it is that of the early Quakers or the Amish, greys and blacks without adornment.

# In the economy of attention the transparent is easily lost.

This sentence is printed in 16 point Bauhaus, the type face from the great protagonists of modern design. Scanning these pages, this will be the sentence that stands out from the 10 point ITC Century font in which the rest of the text is written. With this contrast in form, we are suddenly aware of form as an issue – in this case whether Bauhaus is easier or harder to read than Palatino, and whether it is aesthetically appealing. Like a modern glass window that can change its colour with the sun, we become aware of what we formerly took for granted. We become aware of the issue of style.

To gain attention it is the tradition of rhetoric that comes into play. It is the tradition of Cicero, the speaker or writer who uses many arguments to command a hearing. They are concerned with connecting to their listeners, not with 'empty rhetoric' since that is soon recognised as hollow, but with authenticity presented with style.[2]

An early poster for Cafédirect (shown on the left on page 159) which appeared in colour magazines and on train stations in the South of England in the early 1990s exemplifies this oscillation between substance and style. Its emphasis is on substance – two coffee farmers from San Juan de Loro, an isolated co-op in the Southern mountains of Peru. The farming couple's clothes, the cracked walls of house, and the rough door indicate their circumstances. Their juxtaposition with a modern branded product with the supporting text suggest the directness of Cafédirect and the benefit they would get from the purchase of their coffee. The emphasis here is on the ethical substance of the product. It has a distinctive style in its demonstrable lack of style, and as such it stands in intentional contrast to the overt surface styling of people and products in conventional adverts.[3]

These advertisments put Cafédirect on the map – but it was a restricted map. For the company's market research found that it appealed primarily to those who shared this opposition to style. The research also showed that there was a larger group – up to 30 per cent of consumers – who were sympathetic to the idea of Cafédirect, but who placed the quality of the coffee first. For their attention, the coffee had to taste excellent, and quality had to be the predominant message expressed in the form, with the core ethical content as a supplement.

Environmental ventures and food campaigns have found similar patterns of response. The Canadian energy efficiency programmes began by emphasising the impact of energy retrofits on the environment, but found greater take up when they led with improvements in comfort and the saving in costs, with the $CO_2$ savings as the icing. Similarly with organic food, surveys of purchasers have found that the predominant reason they gave for buying was taste and health rather than the impact of intensive farming on the environment and culture. Each of these will affect the content of the message and its form.

These profiles can change. Those who are primarily concerned with others can grow relative to the ones who are concerned with themselves. But the most powerful message is one that is able to combine the two, that being 'other directed' is part of being 'self directed', that individuality is necessarily social. As the title of a history of the celebrated Peckham health centre experiment put it "Being Me and Also Us".[4] This, of course, touches the very core of social ventures, and how they present themselves to the world – in content as well as form.

Social ventures, particularly those that are tax funded or grant aided, have been suspicious of branding. They prefer service to surface, seeing branding as inauthentic and part of a post modern economy of appearences. Governments find themselves criticised for spending money on branding. Grant givers are reluctant to fund expenditure on brands and all that is involved in developing them. But all ventures have an appearance and a style. It is part of the way they communicate. It is like the mythological shirt of Nessus, the shirt that cannot be torn off. Social ventures should see branding as a flame that indicates a presence and attracts people towards it. It is the first step in widening its connections.

Other reading:
Richard Lanham, The Economy of Attention, University of Chicago Press, 2006

Caroline Wright "Consuming lives, consuming landscapes: interpreting advertisements for Cafédirect coffees" Journal of International Development Volume 16 Issue 5, Pages 665 – 680,2004

End notes

1   On the role of emotion in politics see Drew Weston, The Political Brain, Public Affairs, 2007.
2   An illuminating discussion of the contrast between the philosopher and rhetoritician, and the oscillation between substance and style is in Richard Lanham, The Economy of Attention, University of Chicago Press, 2006. Richard Lanham is a Professor of Medieval Literature and a writer on the new electronic culture.
3   Cafédirect ran a second similar advert at this time which was a portrait of a Nicaraguan woman coffee farmer at work, her face heavily lined. Its strap line ran, "we pay the farmer not the actress" an explicit contrast to a Nestle TV advert running at the same time that associated a stylish woman drinking a cup of Nescafé with seduction by her neighbour from the floor above.
4   Alison Stallibrass, Being Me and Also Us, Lessons of the Peckham Experiment, Scottish Academic Press, 1989.

# 23 OPEN BRANDS

A brand is the way a venture appears to itself and to those around it. It signals visually and in words, the character and values of the organisation. As a form it can attract or repel. It is an affirmation of meaning and the representation of an identity that is seeking connection. In this sense it is an invitation. But as a sign it says nothing about what happens next. It is the type and terms of a resulting connection that matters, and here we see a distinction between closed and open brands.

Green my Apple, to the core.

Greenpeace is a grass roots international movement that relies on the subscriptions of 2.5 million individuals. It campaigns against many forms of environmental pollution and its impact has been achieved by daring, peaceful guerrilla acts such as interfering with whalers, sailing close to nuclear tests, or climbing incinerator chimneys. This has been the substance of its brand.

Accused by its opponents of eco-terrorism, Greenpeace faced a two-thirds fall in its US subscriptions after the 9/11 attacks in New York. In 2006 it responded by experimenting with a new form of 'open' action.

It launched a campaign to persuade Apple to cut toxic materials in its products and to operate a 100 per cent take back recycling service. Taking the Apple brand at its face value, it argued that Apple's generation of toxic waste was at odds with its principles.

Instead of relying on its old model of buccaneering, Greenpeace created an open, viral campaign for its activists. They were encouraged to take action in any way they felt was effective. Some arranged happenings in the Apple shops. Others turned up at (and were turned out of) Macworld trade fairs. They prepared an alternative keynote speech for Steve Jobs that was posted on YouTube which had 100,000 hits before Steve Jobs made his real speech. Activists made their own t-shirts and designs. Two million people sent messages to Steve Jobs. Nine months later Apple announced a change of policy – to phase out its hazardous materials and increase its recycling. Greenpeace had succeeded by 'opening up' its brand.

Much of the distrust of brands is the sense that they have separated form from substance, and that their apparent innocent intimacy is first and foremost instrumental. When these doubts are confirmed the force field of the brand collapses like a soufflé. Firms then have to change their name (like Arthur Andersen Consulting which, after Enron, became Accenture) or are forced to alter those activities that have been exposed (as in the Apple case). So critical is it to retain a perceived connection between brand and substance that many organisations fiercely attack those who question them (large food and catering companies are particularly litigious) and demand control of over all elements of their business.

These points of sensitivity are most acute in relation to the aspects of a product or service that are not tangible to the user. One banana may look much like another, but the chemicals used in their production, and the impact of those chemicals on the land and the labour that produces them is not evident to the shopper. The same is true of the environmental impact and hazards of a product more generally. A user has to trust – in the providers and their regulators. It is trust that is at issue in the brand.

This aspect of a brand is critical for social ventures since their structure and practices are not immediately visible to the user. The organic banana sold through a supermarket relies on its sign – a Soil Association label – to indicate a difference. The story behind a spaghetti made by those with a learning disability on land in Sicily contested by the Mafia can only be alluded to on a label. It is such stories that distinguish so many social projects. As a result social ventures need ways of telling their story. They are restricted by the abbreviations of the normal brand in advertisements and packaging. It is why the fuller coverage of press articles and live television is so important to social ventures, and why the internet opens a new era for the social economy.

Divine chocolate was known by at most two dozen people when it was launched in 1998. It was anonymous on the first day of its appearance in Tesco. Yet by the end of the dance on its first evening BBC's World Channel and 60 journalists all had their story, and two dozen became five million. The internet offers deeper levels of engagement. The Divine website branches into the stories behind it, into details of its structure and its supply chain. Its site for children provides materials for discussion and links to schools in Ghana. And every year cocoa farmers come from Ghana to tell their story all over Britain. If social ventures claim attention by the nature of their narratives, then the internet and its platforms are their home ground for connection. This is the first way in which from the beginning a new venture must go beyond the abbreviation of the brand.

The internet offers a means to go beyond the brand in another way. It provides a way to widen not just understanding but engagement. The Green Apple website (styled like the Mac website) not only presented a story of electronic toxicity and the evidence behind it, it invited its supporters to develop their own means of campaigning. In doing so they played a part in defining the character of Greenpeace in action (the substance), and the way in which Greenpeace appeared to the hundreds of thousands who followed the campaign on sites like YouTube and Flickr (the form). In this case the brand was not a set of images and actions controlled by the centre, but a mosaic of initiatives around a common purpose. This is what we mean by an open brand.

Greenpeace set the object of the campaign. It did the background research and provided materials and ideas to work with. It then acted as a clearing house for the designs and actions developed by its members. The core principles and values which define Greenpeace were the common ground but their interpretation in this case was opened up to members.

There are similar examples which are assisted by but not dependent on the web. Slow Food as it expanded had its own logo (a snail) and system of certification. It had a clear identity and purpose, then found it had attracted a movement around it. But it was complex. It connected people from all over the world, from peasants within the most isolated rural regions to city dwellers. Its founder Carlo Petrini put the organisational problem as follows:

> *"It is precisely in the complexity that we somehow represent so well that we have to find the creative flair and the force to make our demands for better, cleaner and fairer food heard. We must fear the disorder that surrounds us no longer. Precisely the commitment to keep an association as complex as post-Terra Madre Slow Food united has made us realise that we have to put our faith in that disorder. The more we grow as an association, the more we will be disorderly."[1]*

This embracing of disorder, with local convivia determining their own sets of activities and ways they are perceived is the stuff of nightmares for closed organisations. Yet a movement like this is bound together by a common outlook and ethic – developed through periodic gatherings, a web platform, books and an Almanac, and now its own gastonomic university. Like Greenpeace, Slow Food's flame appears as innumerable candles. Its substance and how it appears in everyday practice is shaped by its members.

Both these examples are social movements. But they carry a message for social ventures in considering how to develop a brand and keep it organically connected to their work. Both of them continuously elaborate and extend their content as expressions of their central values and mission, but they gain their strength, their richness and their authenticity from the diversity of activity and expression contributed by their members.

> In developing a venture's brand there are two models. There are closed brands which are tightly controlled from the centre, and which in turn require control of supply chains and all aspects of the operation that relate to the brand. This contrasts with open brands, exemplified in social movements, which invite others to play a part in developing the venture and the way it connects, and is held together by a common core of meaning.

Links
www.greenpeace.org/international/news/greening-of-apple-310507

End notes
1    Carlo Petrini in Slow Food Almanac 2008, Bra 2008, p.7.

# 24 VALUING THE VOLUNTARY

There are divergent views on the role of volunteers for social ventures. Some ventures are largely based on volunteers. Others see the time required to manage them as outweighing any potential benefit, and the effective employment of costless labour as inherently unethical. Volunteerism is seen by some as a threat to properly funded public services and to wages and conditions in the formal sector. It is held to be a principal argument against the informal social economy. But it is a common feature of social ventures that they attract volunteers. For an open organisation they should be a crucial asset. The question is how best to arrange for their participation, how to manage the relations between paid workers and volunteers and how to ensure that both the volunteers and the venture gain from their involvement.

Growing Power, a not for profit land trust, was established in 1995 by former basketball player Will Allen to grow, process, market and distribute healthy food to the residents of Milwaukee.

The two acre urban farm – the organisation's headquarters – includes six greenhouses growing over 12,000 pots of herbs, salads, seedlings, sunflower and radish sprouts; eight hoop-houses for salad greens and vegetables; an apiary; fish; poultry and a wormery; and outdoor pens for livestock including goats, rabbits and turkeys. The farm also includes an anaerobic digester to turn the farm's food waste into energy.

Growing Power sees the farm as an educational lab – and provides hands-on training, demonstrations (as pictured above) and outreach projects to teach and engage the local community. What started as an educational programme where teenagers could work and learn about growing food has grown to cover a number of rural and urban farms in Wisconsin and Illinois. It has a staff of 36 and an army of 2,000 volunteers.

# The new volunteerism

When individuals cross the borders from the household economy into other parts of the social economy without compulsion or contract they take on the classification of the volunteer. The term was initially military and was defined in opposition to the compulsion of conscription (just as voluntary taxation is defined in opposition to the compulsion of taxation). From the 17th century it took a civil form when applied to volunteers for public works or those providing services to the poor.

Just as charitable giving emerged at the same time as the expansion of the market, the concept of the volunteer was the philanthropic shadow to the expansion of wage labour. One concept helped to define the other and legislation together with tax regulations have sought to keep the two categories distinct. Increasingly the boundaries are becoming blurred.

First, there has been a remarkable expansion of the reciprocal economy of the household. We have to remind ourselves that the operating software system of choice in the film industry or for supercomputers, and the basis for a \$36 billion industry of servers, packaged software and desktops is the product of volunteers. Linux, like all open source software, is founded on the voluntary. With the explosive growth of the open source software movement, voluntary labour has ceased to be a poor relation to wage labour. In fact, unpaid reciprocal relationships are proving more powerful innovators in some fields than those based on wage labour.

Linux is closely related to the market. It is used as the basis of proprietary products like RedHat. Its volunteers have jobs. Some firms are even allowing their programmers to contribute to Linux in work time because of what they can learn about the system by the act of contributing. In these cases it is the market that is drawing its nourishment from the household economy, rather than the other way round.

Second, the growth of the cultural economy is marked by an intimate connection of market production and an economy of voluntary enthusiasm. Professional football depends on a global feeder network of amateur leagues where people play and organize for the joy of it. The same is true of many sports, of the music industry, of publishing, and the visual arts. Here enthusiasms may migrate into markets when talent is hired. It also translates into an excess of supply of those wanting to work in the cultural economy and the resulting prevalence of free labour. A succession of internships is now a necessary path to employment in many branches of the sector. But for many the two run side by side, people earning their livelihood in one job to give them time to write, or paint or make music.

Third, the rise in the ratio of dependents to employees means there is a growth in the number of those with the time and interest to follow their enthusiasms and engage in the social world as volunteers. There has been a marked expansion of young volunteers on gap years or after college, and of volunteering by the elderly (in the UK the over 60s contribute some 800 million hours per year in formal voluntary work[1], which at the minimum wage rate would be valued at £4.2 billion p a. In the US the comparable figure for all voluntary work is $18.9 billion).[2]

These three trends have expanded the supply of self directed and voluntary labour and redefined its relation to the market economy from that established four centuries ago. Part of this redefinition involves a dissolution of sharp boundaries between wage and voluntary labour, seeing them rather as two poles in a continuum, along which the two relate in different combinations.

The rise of unemployment, notably amongst the young and the over fifties, interweaves with these trends. The prospect of volunteering becoming a route to paid employment is a real one, and places added importance on the experience and network links that such a volunteer can gain. It also helps that volunteers can be paid (up to £60 a week in the UK without being taxed).

This is part of the continuum from the informal to the formal. Apprentices accept low wages because they are learning. Some full timers move to part time work to give them more time for their own chosen activity whether private (like care in the household) or social (outside). Others may job share or choose less demanding and more flexible wage work to fit in with the work they do voluntarily (the poet U.A. Fanthorpe gave up her job as an English teacher and took one as a hospital clerk to give her more space to write poetry). Many sports and leisure workers work by the season. Overall, full time work between 14 and 60 or 65 which was the norm underlying the welfare institutions of mass production is now breaking up into differentiated work and income earning patterns.

The world of self directed labour is one that has a close affinity to the world of social ventures.

## Ventures and volunteers

Some social mission ventures like Habitat for Humanity are founded on the voluntary principle.[3] Others – like social movements – start as missions or enthusiasms and take on paid staff as they grow in size. Formal ventures are more wary of volunteers and tend to frame their resource needs and shape their structures in terms of paid staffing.

In spite of these differences, three points apply to all social ventures. First, it is in their nature (in contrast to the private market economy) that the venture idea and mission should attract offers of voluntary time and skill. It is a characteristic of successful social ventures and as such, should be seen not as a limitation, but rather as one of its defining advantages.

Second, a new venture should consider how to incorporate and manage voluntary help and support as part of its initial staffing and organizational planning, even if it starts modestly. It may be a question of how to organise well-wishers as friends of the venture, or how to integrate the Board. Or it may be how the social venture can connect with voluntary networks to benefit from their links to users and markets. Or it could apply to interns. In each case the voluntary elements should be part of the venture's organogram not a miscellaneous supplement.

Third, offers of time and skills should be managed as carefully as paid for staff and resources. It is said that Google seeks to treat all its employees as if they were volunteers. A social venture needs to think of its volunteers as if they were employees. There is now a Compact Code of Good Practice for Volunteering in the UK, for example, and a quality standard – Investor in Volunteers – for all organisations that involve volunteers in their work.[4] The standard has ten common sense criteria – for example that volunteers should have defined and rewarding jobs as part of a programme of personal development, that they should be properly managed, and though not paid, their contributions should be recognised.

These would be the kind of criteria for good employment practice for paid employees, but are too often not applied to volunteers. Volunteers tend to be tag-ons, remaining marginalised and consigned to miscellaneous, less skilled jobs. One survey reported that many volunteers ceased volunteering because of a lack of recognition, support, and autonomy, and because they were ill-matched to the tasks they were given.[5] Another survey found that 70 per cent of volunteers said they could have been better organised.[6]

We have found two distinct approaches by social venture managements, which helps explain these findings. One is to see volunteers as a threat to managerial control, lying outside the customary lines and levers of authority. The other is to welcome volunteers as a critical source of innovation and support for ventures with limited financial resources.

In this second approach management is needed – in relation to the identification of modules of work or areas of initiative that can be assigned to volunteers, and the training and support they require. It often helps to have a staff post with primary responsibility for managing volunteers and their interface with the core staff (as the Young Foundation do with their interns) and to ensure that they are included in the living culture of the organisation and its process of formation (**method 20**).

It is not more or less management but rather different styles of management that are at issue. It is the difference between control and mobilization. The authors have witnessed many cases where social ventures managed in the first way have cut themselves off from the resources of a voluntary economy. While there is an overhead and time cost to managing volunteers (one US estimate put it at $300 a volunteer) this is likely to be small relative to the potential benefits of integrating the voluntary economy into the work of a social venture.

The principal benefits are fivefold:

- skills of a level and range that a social venture by itself cannot afford

- sources of innovation

- a staff recruitment pool (as a project grows some volunteers may graduate to paid jobs)

- connectors into a multitude of social networks

- user and market ambassadors.

These are the benefits to the venture. There are also benefits to the volunteer. A social venture offers a volunteer an opportunity to be social in a particular way – to be part of a team that is setting out to create a social project that matters. He or she may also learn, and gain technical experience that is personally useful. But in the end it is the experience of collaborative activity that resonates with people's values – that in the end makes life worth living – which the social venture when it works well can offer to volunteers in whatever way they are able to participate.

In a volunteer economy, roles, relationships and incentives have to be thought about differently from those where there is a contractual wage relationship. If the volunteer receives no payment, then the experience of the work and of contributing to a social goal has to be powerful enough to persuade them to continue. This requires particular managerial and organisational skills, and some overhead expense, but there is great potential value to a new venture if it makes one of its goals the attraction and effective employment of a wide range of volunteers.

**End notes**

1    There is a question about whether such work is adequately described as voluntary. It involves labour certainly – just as shopping or cooking a meal at home is labour – but this is labour that is engaged in not for money but for its own sake, and for what it contributes to the meaning of the lives of those engaged in it. In a sociological sense it is unalienated labour.
2    Sarah Harper, 'Productive Ageing: what do we know' in Geraldine Bedell and Rowena Young (eds) The New Old Age, The Lab, Nesta 2009. This collection outlines arguments and evidence on the value for the elderly of volunteering.
3    Churches have traditionally been run by priests supported by volunteers and there are cases where volunteers have assumed central educational and sacerdotal roles. See for example 'From volunteers to unpaid staff', an interview with Father Leo Bartel, Vicar of the Catholic Diocese of Rockford Illinois, in Peter Drucker, Managing the Nonprofit Organisation, Collins, 1990 pp 161-169.
4    The Compact Code of Good Practice for Volunteering. Available at: http://www.thecompact. org.uk/shared_asp_files/GFSR.asp?NodeID=100323
5    Elisha Evans and Joe Saxton, 'The 21st Century Volunteer: a report on the changing face of volunteering in the 21st Century, nfpSynergy, 2005.
6    Institute for Volunteering Research, the National Survey of Volunteering, 1997

**Links**

www.volunteering.org.uk/
www.growingpower.org

**Reference**

Susan Ellis (ed) The Rants and Raves Anthology: What's on the Minds of Leading Authors in the Volunteer World, energise 2003

# 25 PEOPLE AND PAY

The core of a venture is formed by its contracted staff and elected board. They provide a stability around which relationships can develop. We have already discussed the role of the Board (**method 10**). But what about the staff? What are the structures of pay that reflect the values and mission of the organisation? What does the organisation offer to its staff in terms of prospects and the quality of work? And what role can staff play in extending the ventures mission?

*"It's not just a job I'm doing. It's something I agree with. It's opened my eyes. Now I have my little girl Ria I see more sense to why we are doing it. Since I've started working here and started preaching, a lot of my family have started doing it. Even went to Leicester to see where my sister lives and she's all up for it now separating all her paper from her cardboard and taking everything out of its plastic.*

*I'd like to continue to do something in this field. I go home happy. I've actually done something that's benefited the future. I've always done driving jobs and thought I'm going up the motorway and I'm going to come back and it's getting me nowhere, pointless. Now I have a purpose to get up in the mornings. My outlook has changed."*

These are the words of one of the 73 staff of the Tower Hamlets Community Recycling Consortium, a community enterprise set up to provide a weekly door to door recycling service to the Borough's 73,000 flats, the largest service of its kind in the world. The comments were echoed by many others. The job had a point to it unlike other jobs. They liked the autonomy of the teams, and the control over work that it gave them.

There was a relatively flat pay structure, with the ratio between the highest and lowest limited to 2:1. Work was organised in teams, on a task and finish basis. The somewhat ramshackle depot had a library, an education room (where training and monthly staff meetings took place) and a massage and reflexology room for the staff after work.

The principal constraint in expanding the social economy is not finance but people. There are many ideas, and growing sources of finance ready to back good ideas. But the people to realise them in practice are in short supply.

There is a paradox here, for any thriving social project or enterprise tends to attract large numbers in response to any advertisement. More and more people are looking to work in jobs that have a meaning beyond the pay cheque, like Tower Hamlets recyclers. Often it is people in their late twenties and thirties who may have worked for a decade in mainstream jobs, learning skills and becoming confident of their own capacities, who are looking for work that heals the split between money and values, between the realm of the personal and the world of work.

Some may start their own ventures – and there is a growth of courses and support structures for social entrepreneurs wishing to do so. But there are still too few educational opportunities available in the specific nature and methods of the social economy. By and large these have to be learnt on the job.

## An action academy

We have suggested that a primary staff policy should be formation (**method 20**). Any social venture should see itself first as a form of action academy. Those working there as either paid staff or volunteers should be gaining experience and skills that are valuable not only to themselves and to the venture but to the social economy more generally. Here there is a difference to the private market economy, for in as much as a social venture contributes to the forming of generation of social practitioners it is providing a resource to spread its vision beyond its own boundaries.

Modern public institutions, like the army, the BBC and the NHS, have had an impact of this kind because of their emphasis on training. Many BBC trained engineers for example have left to set up their own firms, and this has resulted in the growth of a substantial industry of small and medium broadcasting electronics companies in the South East. Strong policies of social venture formation can have a similar impact.

From the viewpoint of prospective staff and volunteers a social venture should seek to offer two principal things:

* the participation in realising an idea and the satisfaction that comes from being able to make a recognised contribution

* the scope for developing each person's capacities

From the perspective of the venture, new staff and volunteers offer particular skills and relational capital (namely the relationships they bring with them), and a commitment to take the project forward.

## Tensions

Within this framework, there are four tensions that take a distinct form in social ventures. They are between:

- market rates of pay and the circumstances of the venture's users or suppliers

- paid staff and volunteers

- operations and innovation

- individual development and organisational continuity

## Pay and rations

While the employment and wages policy of a venture should reflect its mission, there are divergent views about how this should be interpreted. One view is that social ventures should have a salary scale similar to that of the private market. It argues that this is necessary to attract the right calibre of people, and because social ventures should not have to rely on lower wages in order to compete.

Our view differs from this. The relevant comparison is not with private market rates of pay but with the circumstances of those to whom the venture's work is directed. The disparity is often most marked in the field of development assistance where a consultant may be paid in a day what those he or she is studying would earn in a year. While there are differences in the cost of living, the basic principle remains that the venture needs to have a moral economy underlying its wage policy, which is seen as fair by all those engaged with the project.[25]

A social venture's wage level relative to the market together with its rate of labour turnover are key indicators of its ability to create a rewarding experience for its staff. There is an inverse relation between the level of wages needed to attract and retain staff on the one hand and the strength of a venture's mission, and the experience of employees on the other. We see this inverse relation in the private sector – at Ferrari in Maranello, for example, where the young mechanics are paid well below market rates but join Ferrari because of its prestige and what they learn from being there. It reflects a general principle in wage theory that firms have to pay a premium if the work lacks meaning (one of the foundation stones of Taylorism was that a worker should be paid a higher wage for agreeing to be deskilled and the resultant loss of autonomy). Social ventures should not have to pay that premium.

The point applies equally to relative wages within a venture. The 2:1 ratio in the case of the Tower Hamlets Community Recycling Consortium is not uncommon in worker co-ops. 3:1 is a more typical benchmark in the community sector. It is not that staff in a venture should not be paid a living wage. Rather it is to introduce the notion of equity as perceived both by staff, volunteers, and the users (or in the fair trade case the suppliers) in the comparative levels of pay. Where problems arise is when some staff are paid at market rates (because their skills are said to be needed) while others are paid at the levels of the moral economy. This is a divisive practice that will weaken any such organisation.

In business and public organisations a common finding of research is that the more people know about others' pay the more dissatisfied they are likely to be. Few people believe that it's fair for them to be paid less than others. But in organisations with a social mission this pattern is less common. One strategy that has helped resolve pay tensions internally is full wage transparency. This approach was introduced by the think tank Demos. It caused initial unease, and there were some immediately recognized anomalies. But once these had been redressed, the practice ensured a great sense of equity. A similar practice was followed by the School of Everything.

## Paid staff and volunteers

The question of the perceived fairness of rates of pay is particularly relevant for the relations of a venture to its volunteers. The more the levels of pay diverged from an equity norm, the greater the disincentive to the volunteer.

A good example is Oxfam whose network of 900 shops has 20,000 volunteers to run them. Oxfam exemplify the approach outlined in **method 24**. They have a clear code for volunteers and a commitment to provide them with the necessary skills. Ten years ago this voluntary retail economy was thrown into crisis by the appointment of 500 managers to run the busiest shops. The managers were recruited at a salary level that the volunteers considered to be out of proportion to the ethic and goals of the organisation. The restoration of the fortunes of the shops and the fact that the managers helped them generate income to fund Oxfam's aid programmes restored a measure of stability.

The incipient tension that arises between paid and unpaid staff can be lessened in a variety of ways: first and foremost by recognition of the volunteer's contribution, but also by tangible reciprocity (one unpaid board member of a small real ale company told us he valued his monthly crate of beer more than many times is monetary value). There is also the possibility discussed in **method 24** of nominal payments, whether in cash or – in some places – local currency notes. All this can be summarized in the dictum that volunteers should not be taken for granted.

## Operations and innovation

In all productive organisations there is also a potential tension between operations and innovation. The incessant demands of running anything crowd out time and creative space to radically innovate. This is why it often takes the disruption of a major crisis to force an organisation to change. One of the authors has vivid memory of a remarkable doctor in his Devon surgery discussing practice innovation in the new PFI-funded surgery under the reproving eye of the practice general manager for whom running the existing practice was more than enough.

This tension at its core is one of function not of people. It is nevertheless expressed through people, and erupts in many different forms: the innovator replaced in a coup by disturbed investors; a board concerned that its chief executive is so busy in pursuing the policy of openness that he or she does not have his or her eye on the main business; the operational manager impatient with what he or she experiences as the lack of grip of the chief executive; all those in the existing operations resentful that they are left with the mundane jobs while new ventures have the exciting ones and that the resources the existing services have generated are being devoured in risky initiatives.

These are all factors that act as a drag on innovative social organisations remaining so. When faced with the problems, boards tend to side with operations for there is nothing that traditional boards dislike more than the sense that organisations for which they have responsibility are in any sense chaotic. Whether in large organisations or small, where there is much to lose as well as to gain, the tendency will be to appoint the competent operational manager as the Chief Executive with the innovator as subordinate rather than the other way round.

Our view is that ventures need to recognize this emerging tension from the beginning – in their innovation phase – and plan their structure and staffing to take this into account. If the venture is to remain innovative then it must institutionalize the space and capacity to innovate – through the open policies (**method 18**) and reflective formation (**method 20**) approaches outlined earlier, through earmarked funding and spin-offs (as well as spin-ins), through sticking with innovative chief executives but with an operational deputy in charge of the day to day, supported by sophisticated operational systems.

## Individual development and organizational continuity

Social ventures depend on continuity for the strength of their relationships, yet individuals gain from mobility. This has always been a problem for family firms – where children can learn the trade from their parents, but need a wider perspective if they are to progress. In the furniture industrial district of Jutland in Western Denmark, sons went to the local technical college, were then sent on a ten years plus tour of Western Europe, working in different furniture factories, to return with this knowledge and contacts to take over from the father when he retired. High-tech firms encourage their employees to move and return, or to work part time so that they gain experience elsewhere.

Social ventures need to retain this perspective for their employees. They should plan for moves and secondments to widen experience while retaining the staff connection to the home base. Like alumni, former employees should be welcomed back to events that helps retain continuity with users and suppliers. It is part of a strategy for expanding relational capital.

Developing its staff is important not only for the venture itself but to create a group of individuals able to put the ideas into practice more widely. In its internal policies the structures of pay and its operational practices should reflect the venture's mission, and avoid the tensions that can arise between market rates of pay and what is considered equitable with respect to all staff, volunteers and the venture's beneficiaries. It should also foresee the further common tension between the demands of operational management and the conditions for continuing innovation.

# A BRIEF BIBLIOGRAPHY

There is a growing literature of books by pioneers of social ventures. They are remarkable narratives, containing many ideas and lessons for those engaged in social venturing. There are striking similarities in the kinds of obstacles and hostilities that they often meet with and how they are dealt with. They also show an inversion of customary ways of doing things, that have led to so many radical technological and organisational innovations.

## Autobiographies and biographies of social ventures

Saul Alinsky, Reveille for Radicals, Vintage, 1969
Ibrahim Abouleish, Sekem: a Sustainable Community in the Desert, Floris, 2004
Ela Bhatt, We are Poor But So Many, Oxford, 2006
Augusto Boal, Legislative Theatre, New York, Routledge, 1998
Pooran Desai and Sue Riddlestone, BioRegional Solutions for Living on One
    Planet, Green Books, 2003
Danilo Dolci, The Outlaws of Partinico, MacGibbon and Kee, 1960
Masanobu Fukuoka, The One-Straw Revolution, Rodale Press, 1978
Dee Hock, One from Many, Visa and the Rise of Chaordic Organisation,
    Berrett-Koehler, 2005
Harriet Lamb, Fighting the Banana Wars & Other Fair Trade Battles, Rider, 2008
Carlo Petrini, Slow Food Revolution, Rizzoli International, 2006
Abdul Sattar Edhi, A Mirror to the Blind, A.Sattar Edhi Foundation, 2006
Andrew Mawson, The Social Entrepreneur: Making Communities Work,
    Atlantic Books, 2008
M.P. Parameswaran, Democracy by the People: the Elusive Kerala Experience,
    Alternatives Asia, 2008
Ian Smillie, Freedom from Want, The Remarkable Story of BRAC, Kumarian, 2009
Tim Smit, Eden, Chartered Institute of Personnel and Development, 2005
Mierle Laderman Ukeles, "On Maintenance and Sanitation Art" in Tom
    Finkelpearl (ed) Dialogues in Public Art, MIT Press, 2001.
Hilary Wainwright, Public Service Reform But Not as We Know it, Picnic, 2009
    (the story of change in IT systems in Newcastle City Council).
Muhummad Yunus, Banker to the Poor, Aurum Press, 2003
Muhammad Yunus, Creating a World Without Poverty, Public Affairs, 2007

## Other books on social ventures

David Bornstein, How to Change the World, Oxford University Press, 2007
Peter Drucker, Managing the Nonprofit Organisation, Collins, 1990
John Elkington and Pamela Hartigan, The Power of Unreasonable People,
    Harvard Business Press, 2008

## And for more technical discussions:

John Carver, Boards that Make a Difference, 3rd edition, Jossey-Bass, 2006
J. Gregory Dees, Jed Emerson and Peter Economy, Strategic Tools for Social
Entrepreneurs, Wiley, 2002 (this is one of a large series by Wiley on managing
    social ventures)